12
STUPID
MISTAKES
people make with their
Money

12 STUPID MISTAKES

people make with their

Money

by

Dan Benson

W PUBLISHING GROUP™

www.wpublishinggroup.com

A Division of Thomas Nelson, Inc.
www.ThomasNelson.com

CONTENTS

Are You Making a Stupid Money Mistake?

*If you find yourself in a hole, the first thing to
do is stop digging.*

—WILL ROGERS

Wow, do I need that book!"

"How soon will it be ready? I want copies for my kids—and for *their* kids!"

Quite often, after a speaking engagement or media interview related to my earlier books on personal finance, people ask me about my next project. During the past year, I've been telling them about *12 Stupid Mistakes People Make with Their Money*, and the response has been electric:

"I could be your cover model for stupid money mistakes!" one interviewer offered.

"Did I ever need that book when I graduated from college!" an audience member reflected.

You work hard to provide life's necessities . . . to pay monthly bills and supply needs and wants . . . to handle unexpected financial emergencies . . . to provide for your children's college and wedding expenses . . . and to save and invest for a meaningful retirement. You want financial freedom—who doesn't? But succeeding with your money is one of life's biggest challenges because there are so many ways to "blow it," so many pitfalls along the path to financial freedom.

You've undoubtedly stumbled into a few of those traps yourself. As a former financial planner, I've seen the damage caused by twelve all-too-typical mistakes people make with their money. Stupid mistakes, really. Little boo-boos that can postpone goals. Big blunders that can devastate dreams. Common missteps that otherwise intelligent, well-meaning individuals and couples easily, frequently make with their money. It's not that these good people are stupid; they've simply made some *stupid money decisions*. And there's a big difference. The folks I quoted earlier were indeed wise to recognize that they'd slipped up and needed some guidance. It happened to be my privilege to show them how to pull themselves from the trap, dust themselves off, and start anew on the road to financial freedom—smarter, wiser, more hopeful about their financial futures, and a bit shrewder about the inevitable traps waiting for them down the road.

How to Attain Good Judgment

I would be dishonest if I were to pretend that I have not made any of these Stupid Mistakes myself. I have. I'm reminded of the ambitious young man who interviewed the successful senior citizen:

"Tell me, sir, how did you attain all your good judgment?"

"From experience."

"And where did you attain your experience?"

"From bad judgment."

Indeed, if experience and bad judgment are good teachers, then I should be wise beyond my years. Much of what I now do right I first did wrong, and there isn't an honest financial adviser in the world who would tell you differently. So if you count yourself among the hapless souls who feel they can be poster children for the 12 Stupid Money Mistakes, please do not feel ashamed or that all hope is lost.

In fact, I'm very encouraged at your realization that perhaps you've made a mistake or two along the way . . . and that you may be susceptible to mistakes in the future. I'm encouraged that you want to learn smart ways to avoid the Stupid Mistakes, smart ways to manage and invest your money more productively, smart ways to indeed get your ducks in a row so you can:

- handle future emergencies such as unexpected job layoffs, car or home repairs, and medical expenses;

- provide for your children's college education, wedding expenses, and other important family goals; and

- enjoy a financially secure retirement in which you can live out your dreams.

The Journey to Financial Freedom

I'm here to tell you that you, too, can extricate yourself from the money traps of your past, dust yourself off, and begin again your journey to financial freedom with a level of wisdom and confidence greater than ever before.

That's why I take delight in preparing this book for you, for your present or future spouse, and for your present or future children. In the following pages you're going to discover twelve of the most common mistakes good people make with their money . . . the havoc or lost opportunity each Stupid Mistake can wreak in your financial life . . . smart ways to avoid those traps in the future . . . and, most important, the amazing benefits to your finances—and indeed, your life—as you steer clear of the 12 Stupid Mistakes and build a solid financial future.

For example . . .

- When you learn to avoid Stupid Mistake #2, you will no longer be caught like a deer in headlights whenever a financial emergency crests the hill. Your next out-of-the-blue car repair or medical copayment will be far more manageable. Even a job layoff will be less stressful. (Notice I didn't say *fun*. Just less stressful—for you and your pocketbook.)

- Steer clear of Stupid Mistake #4, and you'll *save hundreds of dollars—more likely thousands—this year alone*. It can mean saving *tens of thousands* over a lifetime, dollars you can put to work building financial independence.

- If you break free of Stupid Mistake #5, you'll regain control of hundreds of dollars each month—"found money" that will help you free up your cash flow and save for future needs and dreams. Investing this money instead of washing it down the drain could make you $150,000 *richer* twenty years from now.

By now I hope you're beginning to see that this book is not simply a lament over the costly mistakes people make with their money. Will Rogers's homespun wisdom is just as appropriate today as it was in his time: "If you find yourself in a hole, the first thing to do is stop digging." If you find yourself in the hole with one or more of these mistakes, my goal is to help you stop digging and turn your financial life around. And if you're fortunate enough to have steered clear of the holes to this point, I want to prepare you with the knowledge and insight to avoid those costly traps in the future.

- You may not think Stupid Mistake #6 is a financial issue—until you begin paying its high cost. This trap will not only cost you thousands of dollars, it will also deteriorate *your job capability* and *your overall quality of life*. We'll pinpoint ten key strategies for steering clear of this common pitfall.

- Stupid Mistake #7 could mean the difference between *striving* or *thriving* financially in your retirement years. Keep digging this hole, and you may as well plan on moving in with your kids. But heed the guidance in this crucial chapter, and you can build the financial freedom to *enjoy the retirement of your dreams*.

- I call Stupid Mistake #8 "extreme investing" for good reason: *Many of us invest either too fearfully or too aggressively*. Fear can cause us to keep our money in ultraconservative investments that barely keep up with inflation; fear can also cause us to "invest with the lemmings" and buy and sell our investments at precisely the wrong time. On the other hand, if we invest too aggressively, we seek high returns at too high a risk. (Everyone who was heavily invested in technology stocks or technology mutual funds in early 2000 knows too well the heart-stopping losses that can result from this form of extreme investing.) In this chapter I'll show you how to design *an investment plan that avoids the extremes and enhances your opportunity for steady growth*.

- Allow Stupid Mistake #10 into your life, and it may not let you go. Unfortunately, this one has become more and more prevalent over the past decade; it is not only a drain on your own financial resources, but it is also a terrible disservice to your children. Its negative impact can affect multiple generations. The good news is that *you can totally avoid this mistake*—if you have the courage to do so.

These are just a few samples of the discoveries that await you as we visit together in the coming pages. So find a pen or highlighter (go ahead; I'll wait), then turn the page and see if you recognize someone you know in *12 Stupid Mistakes People Make with Their Money*.

Yours for financial freedom,
DAN BENSON

Counting on the Illusive "Someday"

*The best time to plant an oak tree is twenty
years ago. The next-best time is now.*

— DAVID CHILTON, *The Wealthy Barber*

Someday I'm going to get out of debt."

"When I get my next raise, then . . ."

"Maybe after Christmas I can start saving."

"Someday, when our ship comes in . . ."

If you've caught yourself entertaining such thoughts recently, welcome to the club. Ours is a culture of financial discontent. Like everyone else, you probably make enough to "get by" each month, maybe even make payments on an extra vehicle or two or tuck away a few dollars in the company retirement plan. But you dream of a better, brighter financial future. A time when cash flow isn't so tight, when you have savings and investments to cover needs and dreams. A time when you can say good-bye to fifty-hour work weeks and "graduate" to a retirement in which you're financially free to live the adventures you've always wanted to live. And as you envision these things, you sense a nervous, nagging feeling, deep inside, that there is much more you should be doing if you're ever going to move beyond "getting by" and enjoy a life of financial freedom.

You want to, but you don't know how. You're aware of some crucial steps you need to take, but with your present-day obligations you don't see how you can possibly do so.

So you lapse into the illusive "Someday."

Maybe your consumer debts are piled high: Despite good intentions, you've put too many expenditures on credit cards and now the payments are draining your monthly cash flow. *How did those balances get so high so fast? Cash is tight, so I'll just make minimum payments for now. Someday . . .*

You may be among the millions whose savings accounts aren't where they need to be. Maybe you had to drain your savings to pay for an emergency and haven't been able to pay yourself back. Or perhaps you raided savings to handle another "emergency" such as a new sound system (got to have that MX-57 Master-Blaster Surround Sound with Quadruple Earthquake Woofers) or riding mower (everyone else on our street has one) or expensive vacation (we deserved it). You were going to rebuild that rainy-day account quickly, but real life and its related expenses overwhelmed your good intentions. Or maybe, like millions of others, you've just never been able to save successfully in the first place. *If only I made more money. When I get my next raise, maybe then . . .*

Your kids are growing fast; it won't be long until they're ready for college. Will you be? During the next decade a four-year public-university education is expected to cost $40,000—double that for a private college. By the year 2018, pundits are saying, four years at a public college or university could run $100,000 and a private college nearly $200,000. Intimidating, isn't it? *Can't do much right now . . . but someday our ship will come in. Maybe an inheritance from Mom and Dad . . .*

As quickly as the kids have grown older, so have you. We don't like to admit that or give in to it; that's why hair coloring, tooth whitening, plastic surgery, vitamin supplements, health clubs, home-fitness machinery, and Viagra do land-office business among today's aging baby boomers. Suddenly, we realize that our lives are most likely half over. That the time is rapidly approaching when either we or our employers will say "Time to hang 'em up," and the steady paycheck will be suddenly replaced by a card and a pen-and-pencil set. But how many of us will be financially ready? One recent study reported that 60 percent of baby boomers in their forties think they could personally face a retirement savings crisis. Will you? *Can't do much now. But once we get the kids through school, then we can save for retirement. Besides, there's Social Security, and probably an inheritance . . .*

Someday. It's human nature's way of acknowledging guilt without repenting and changing our ways. It's like saying "I'll stop procrastinating tomorrow." But like tomorrow, Someday never arrives. There's no date on the calendar called "Someday." It's just a hazy, shapeless, undefined concept in time—always out there somewhere in the nebulous future, as far away as we can mentally push it so that we won't have to think about it. "Someday thinking" enables us to continue our nonproductive or counterproductive courses by assuring ourselves of good intentions to do better . . . later.

Someday's High Cost

Why are we citing Someday thinking as one of the 12 Stupid Mistakes people make with their money? Because Someday thinking leads to procrastination, and *procrastination is easily the number-one, most common, most damaging blunder you can possibly make with your money*. If you put off until Someday what you could and should be doing today, you will pay a steep price indeed. Check out Jack and Jill:

- Jack, 50, who always knew that Someday he should begin saving for his retirement years, has finally realized that he'd better turn someday into today—and fast. He determines to set aside $300 each month in his company's 401(k) plan. Assuming Jack works sixteen more years to age 66, and that his investments within the 401(k) grow an average of 10 percent per year over those sixteen years, Jack will have $141,131 when he retires. Sounds like a big sum now, but how long will that amount last when Jack is no longer working? Three, maybe four years?

- Jill, 30, started her own 401(k) contributions this year, also contributing $300 per month. If Jill also works to age 66, averages the same 10 percent on her investments, and never contributes more than $300 per month, she will retire with $1,262,028 in her retirement fund. Same monthly contribution, same return on investment. The difference? Time. Jill didn't fall victim to Stupid Mistake #1, Counting on the Illusive "Someday." Instead, she made the commitment twenty years earlier than Jack to save the same amount. *The difference: $1,120,897.*

Someday and Your Credit Cards

Another area in which Someday thinking costs dearly is credit card debt. Today the average American family carries balances totaling more than $8000 on fourteen credit cards, and more offers for more credit cards arrive in the mail every week. Whenever you place an expense on a credit card, you procrastinate payment for the item or service you've purchased. It's one thing to know you have the cash set aside to pay in full when the bill arrives, but if you procrastinate payment beyond the grace period, then interest accrues on the unpaid balance. This is delightful to the credit card issuer, but a big, stupid mistake on the part of the credit cardholder. An $8000 credit card balance, at 16.9 percent annual interest, costs $1352 per year. At 19.9 percent, it's $1592. Now observe Brittany and Ted:

- Brittany has heeded the call of consumerism: "Buy now, pay forever." Some of her credit card purchases have already been consumed (vacation, dinners out, hair and nail salon, gasoline); others have depreciated in value (CD player, CDs, furniture, Home Shopping Network gotta-have-its). And instead of paying these purchases in full when her card statements arrived, she procrastinated payment. "Someday," she said. Just what the credit card issuers wanted to hear. They'll make nearly $1500 in interest *this year alone* from Brittany's procrastination. Meanwhile Brittany's debt service of $400 per month (of which nearly $125 is interest) wreaks havoc with her monthly cash flow.

- Ted, on the other hand, doesn't believe in Someday thinking. His income is similar to Brittany's, but he spends according to plan from his cash allotment or checking account, saves in advance for larger purchases, and if he should use his one and only credit card, he pays off the balance in full as soon as the statement arrives. Credit card issuers don't like Ted as much as they like Brittany, although that doesn't stop them from trying. But Ted shreds every credit card sales pitch upon arrival; his one no-fee card is all he'll ever need, thank you. Since he carries no consumer debt, Ted can take the same amount Brittany spends in debt service and invest it each month in a mutual fund. If that fund averages just 8 percent over the next three years, Ted will have added $16,214 to his nest egg. Meanwhile, Brittany will be continuing to flush away hundreds each month, thousands each year, still and forever paying for those consumed and depreciated purchases.

You May Be Making Stupid Mistake #1 If . . .

o you find yourself counting on a raise to break even

o you're putting off saving or paying off debts until a "better day"

o you hope Mom and Dad leave you a nice inheritance

o you catch yourself thinking, *If only I made more money*

o you play Lotto or otherwise long for your ship to come in

"If Only I Made More Money . . ."

Jeff and MaryAnn were Someday thinkers. In their midthirties, they had one elementary-age child and earned an above-average income. They had suffered no devastating setbacks. Yet financially they were barely keeping their heads above water. When they came to see me and pulled out a list of their monthly expenses, I could see frustration in their eyes.

"We work so hard, it seems we should have more to show for it," Jeff said. "But our monthly expenses wipe out about everything."

"We'd really like to be putting some aside for retirement and for Amanda's college education," MaryAnn joined in. "Really, we just need breathing room. But with all our monthly expenses and then insurance and Christmas and birthdays, there just isn't enough. If only we made more money . . ."

5

If only. Jeff and MaryAnn were stuck on a paycheck-to-paycheck treadmill. It didn't take an accounting degree to quickly see that they had chosen a high-expense, credit-driven lifestyle that demanded inordinate proportions of each month's available cash. But because they had identified their problem as insufficient income, the only solution they could see was to *make more money.* Such longing is a common manifestation of Someday thinking: We can't imagine restructuring our financial priorities, and we don't want to face the "pain" of disciplined spending and saving, so let's hope that someday we'll make more money.

I told Jeff and MaryAnn about Parkinson's Second Law.

In 1960 a book titled *The Law and the Profits* swept management circles around the world. Its author was C. Northcote Parkinson, who is still widely quoted today because of a shrewd observation that would become famous as Parkinson's Law: *Work expands to fill the time available.*

This principle underscores a universal truth that workers had always suspected but were embarrassed to verbalize: that no matter how much time you're able to save in the workplace, your workload will always increase to fill the time you thought you had saved. What many people don't remember is that within the same book, Parkinson made a second statement that in my view is even more timely and prophetic than the first: *Expenditures rise to meet income.*

Think about that for a moment. Have you ever promised yourself, "After my next raise, I'm going to pay off my bills and start saving more . . ." only to see your personal expenses rise to consume the amount of the raise? You're not abnormal or alone; this happens every day. Parkinson knew human nature well. He went on to say, *Individual expenditure not only rises to meet income but tends to surpass it, and probably always will.* In other words, by the time any extra income happens along, we already have a list of plans for it.

Jeff and MaryAnn's problem was not their income level. Their true problem was they had literally "bought in" to America's get-it-now, do-it-now syndrome, which drove them to spend everything they made, and then some, in conformance to Parkinson's Second Law. Without a major turnabout in their financial priorities and practices, "more money" would only continue to be consumed by higher expenditures. Therefore, Jeff and MaryAnn's Someday thinking regarding "more money" was not the answer to their dilemma but simply a smokescreen to mask their need for an intervention in their financial decision making.

I assured Jeff and MaryAnn that they were neither abnormal nor alone. Indeed, theirs is the financial road most traveled in our world—the path of too-easy credit, of instant gratification with the newest and best, of putting off what should be done while longing and hoping for a mythical ship to come in. I also assured them that this path of least resistance can be a slippery slope of financial despair. With my encouragement, they resolved to back up and choose a surer path. Together, we turned bad habits into good habits, and before long Jeff and MaryAnn were well along the road to financial freedom. They learned

that *it's not how much you make, but what you do with what you make* that makes all the difference.

"Someone Else Will Take Care of Me . . ."

Few people have the nerve to state this aloud, but, deep down, millions hold this Someday fantasy in the back of their minds. It comes from the old-school, outmoded mind-set that as we grow older we'll be financially cared for by our government, our former employers, or inheritances from our parents or a long-lost rich aunt. And if none of those come through, we can always move in with our adult children.

"Someday I'll Get Social Security . . ."

America's Social Security system was born in 1935 as a federal initiative to help bring the country out of the Great Depression. Its purpose was to provide an incentive for workers to leave the labor pool at age sixty-five, thus leaving their jobs open for the droves of younger adults who were urgently searching for work.

But in 1935 the average life expectancy was sixty-three, so our benevolent government figured that starting payouts at age sixty-five was a fairly safe commitment to make. Even those who made it to age sixty-five were likely, on average, to survive just four or five more years. The government's promise was doubly conservative because during the system's first ten years, more than forty workers contributed to the system for every one retiree drawing a stipend. The maximum annual contribution was $30.

Today life spans have increased to the point that a typical retiree may draw benefits for fifteen to thirty years instead of just four or five. Now there are only three workers supporting every retiree, and the Social Security board of trustees projects that by the year 2025 the ratio could be as low as two workers per beneficiary. Social Security taxes keep going up as payouts grow larger and Congress indexes benefits to inflation. In addition, benefits have been expanded to include health and disability insurance.

As a result, every few years a watchdog group proclaims that the Social Security system will go bankrupt within the next few decades, leaving today's younger baby boomers and Gen Xers in the lurch when they reach retirement age. One recent survey reported that more men and women under the age of thirty-four believe more readily in UFOs than in the availability of a Social Security stipend when they grow older.

I do not share the view that Social Security will go under, for the simple reason that congressmen and -women and presidents like to stay in office. The senior voting bloc, already powerful in Washington, will grow even stronger as 76 million baby boomers begin joining its ranks over the next several years. Politicians know a big voting bloc when they see one, so to court the senior vote they'll keep the system struggling along by continuing to increase the Social Security tax, pushing the qualification ages higher, and possibly instituting some form of privatization—all while screaming that the other party doesn't care about senior citizens.

But even though Social Security may indeed be there for you, what should you plan on? Not much. It's crucial to recognize that Social Security was never designed to be a "retirement plan" or the sole source of one's retirement income. It was established to serve only as *a supplement, a safety net.* Today it provides less than one-fourth of most retirees' monthly income needs. Here's why: If you were to qualify for the full Social Security pension today, you would receive approximately $12,000 per year per working person—half that for a spouse who hasn't accrued sufficient Social Security credits. Sure, $12,000 helps, but it won't provide the life you want to live after you stop full-time work. I usually suggest that today's midlifers plan on receiving approximately one-half that amount, or $6,000 per year. I hope I'm wrong and that the system thrives in the future, but I'd rather err on the side of caution. Many financial planners go so far as to counsel clients to work, save, and invest as though

Social Security won't be there at all. You can't go wrong that way, and this book is geared to show you how to do just that. Then, if Social Security income happens to be there for you in the future, you can regard it as icing on the cake. The bottom line is that Social Security is in the hands of politicians, which means that it'd be another Stupid Mistake to rely heavily on the system for your retirement years.

"Someday I'll Get a Pension . . ."

In days of old, the typical corporate pension was the defined-benefit package, in which the company funded the plan for you, took responsibility for managing its investments, and, upon vesting, guaranteed you a specific monthly pension upon your retirement.

But in recent years this has shifted dramatically. The old pensions assumed mutual loyalty and long tenures between employers and employees—two qualities that, to our discredit, can no longer be counted on. Downsizings, buyouts, new technologies, and tough times have made corporations more likely to turn employees loose before the employees are fully vested in their pension plans. Likewise, unlike our parents' generation, it's rare for today's employee to stay with the same company for an entire career. Such mobility makes defined-benefit pensions cumbersome to administer and difficult to benefit from. Another factor in the decline of such pensions is that horror stories abound of pension funds disappearing into fiscal sinkholes—and former employees suing their companies for mismanagement or fraud. Fewer and fewer companies want to bear responsibility for the performance of a pension fund's underlying investments. Thus, defined-benefit pensions are becoming either obsolete or difficult to count on.

"Someday, When I Get My Inheritance . . ."

Our parents' generation built assets of $10.4 trillion, which will soon begin to be passed on to us, their adult children. But not all of our parents participated equally in the post–World-War-II boom, and neither will we share equally in the future transfer of wealth. There may be an inheritance in your future or maybe not. However, it's unwise to count on an inheritance because there are simply too many unknowns. You may not know your parents' fiscal situation and may find it awkward to ask; even if you ask, they may not want to tell; and no one can predict how long they'll live, what their future expenses will be, or how much of their asset bases will remain once they are gone.

And there's a deeper, more visceral reason why I discourage anyone from relying on an inheritance. I hold a strong conviction that an inheritance is not an obligation, but a *gift*. It's our parents' hard-earned money, not ours. They've already given us far more than we can ever repay. As they grow older, they deserve to enjoy financial freedom and live out their dreams with absolutely no pressure, spoken or implied, to leave some for us.

In my opinion, it's sad commentary that many of today's middle-age adults seem to regard an inheritance as an entitlement. I'm disgusted whenever I hear presumptuous, boomer-age children bemoaning the fact that "Mom and Dad are out spending *our* money."

Hello? It's not our money. It may never be. It belongs to our parents. Contrary to popular thought, we do not *deserve* it. Therefore, it's not only boorish but also stupid to plan on it.

Kathy and I have tried to remove any inheritance pressure from our parents by assuring them that we hope they spend their last dollar the day they die. In other words: It's theirs to use to live life to the full! We don't want them to scrimp during their senior years just to pass something along to us. If they do leave us something when they pass away, of course we'll be grateful. But we will look upon any such bequest as *an unexpected gift, not an entitlement*. It's certainly not an obligation on their part, for our parents have already given us far more than money and far more than we deserve.

If you've ever found yourself counting on a potential inheritance from your parents, I hope you will reexamine your heart. It's not *your* inheritance. It's not your money. It's theirs. Encourage them to use it to make the most of the rest of their lives. Meanwhile, chart your own course so you can do the same.

The Future Is Now

I've placed Someday thinking, and the baggage that comes with it, at the top of our list of 12 Stupid Mistakes for a very important reason: Counting on the illusive "someday" lies at the very core of financial failure. As we have seen, Someday thinking leads to wishing, longing, and procrastination—all of which are weak attempts to remove fiscal responsibility from ourselves and place it upon someone or something else.

But the fact is, you can't count on the illusive Someday. Wishful thinking, fantasizing, and procrastination will cost you big-time. Longing for "more money" is empty whining unless you also commit to shifting your priorities. Hoping to be bailed out by Social Security or a corporate-paid pension or a big inheritance is a loser's game. No one else is going to build financial independence for you.

It's up to you.

The future is not "someday." The future is now.

Stupid Mistake #2

Waiting till It Pours to Realize You Don't Have an Umbrella

It wasn't raining when Noah built the ark.

- Your teenaged daughter takes the car on a quick errand. Just to the drugstore and back, she assures you. Then you get the phone call. "Mom, you know the intersection of Third and Main? I was, like, going through the intersection, and the light turned too fast. Like, it went right from green to red. Well, like, the new car kinda has a big dent in it."

- You've been working fifty-plus hours per week for as long as you can remember. When you're not on the job you're thinking about it or losing sleep over it. You desperately need a vacation—not a few days off to paint the deck, but a genuine, get-outta-town, mind-in-neutral, no-visiting-the-parents vacation to rejuvenate the mind, body, and soul. But to do it right would cost $1000 minimum—more like $2500 if you want to eat, sleep on a mattress, and use fixtures with plumbing—and the money just isn't there.

- "We'll just run some tests," your doctor says. "Your insurance should cover it." Sixty days later you receive a not-so-friendly statement announcing that the total for your procedures was $526.28, of which your health insurer has now paid its generous share, $28.78. The remaining $497.50 is up to you—and thirty days past due.

- Your father passed away a few years back and your mother's vitality is failing. Soon she'll need to move to a retirement center and perhaps its assisted-living facility. But her financial reserves are limited. She's going to need help with the up-front costs and with her monthly expenses. You love her dearly and want to help. But with your present family obligations, where will you find the extra money?

- Your supervisor calls you into her office and shuts the door. There's a tense, pregnant silence as she takes her place behind her desk. "As you know, we've had a tough year," she begins. You shift nervously. So does she. "And we've reached a point at which we have to cut back and let some people go. Yours is one position we have to downsize. You'll receive two weeks' severance."

One Thing Is Certain: Life Is Uncertain

Costly emergencies. Care for an aging parent. Loss of your job. No doubt you've encountered some of these financial storms already. Somewhere in your future, they'll dump on you again. We all know we can't keep life's storm clouds from raining on us; they're an inevitable, unavoidable part of walking this earth. If one thing is certain, it's that life is uncertain. Each morning we rise from our beds not knowing what challenges will come our way. But we've been around the block enough to know that real life is not all pleasant breezes and blue skies. Skies darken. Lightning strikes.

And life's storms often cost money. Sometimes big money.

Despite all of your hard work, current income does not always meet current expenses. Life's little and not-so-little financial surprises just do not time themselves to fit neatly within your income streams or monthly cash flow. When you're trying to stay solvent from month to month, working hard just to keep up with the ever-increasing cost of living, let alone to save for long-term needs such as your retirement years, those storms can wreak havoc on your best-laid plans.

Acknowledging the potential of life's certain uncertainties underscores the importance of being better prepared financially so that we can weather those storms without getting buried in debt, depleting retirement savings, losing our homes, or having to mooch from our family and friends. It means buying a good umbrella before the deluge hits. Financial emergencies are never fun, but at least we can be better prepared so that we control the financial outcome instead of letting circumstance determine our destinies.

But alas, you do not live among the most prudent of savers. In the most prosperous country in the world, the average American household sets aside less than 4 percent of its gross income for long-term and short-term savings combined. As I write this, Americans collectively have spent more than they earn over the past six months, virtually relegating savings to an afterthought. The wise author of the ancient proverb must have foreseen our contemporary mind-set when he wrote: "The wise man saves for the future, but the foolish man spends whatever he gets. . . . A prudent man foresees the difficulties ahead and prepares for them; the simpleton goes blindly on and suffers the consequences (Proverbs 21:20; 22:3 TLB).

Foolish man. Simpleton. In today's language, *stupid*. That ancient proverb holds true for us today: 'Tis a stupid mistake to spend everything we make and not set aside a reserve for the difficulties ahead.

It's not that most of us don't *want* to save for the future, or that we don't realize the need to do so. Rather, we allow too many other things to wedge their ways topward on our priority lists.

It's Parkinson's Second Law, which we visited in Chapter 1: *Expenditures rise to meet income. Individual expenditure not only rises to meet income, but tends to surpass it, and probably always will.*

Take George, for example.

"There Just Isn't Anything Left to Save!"

George contends that he makes just enough to get by—that after his regular monthly expenses, "There just isn't anything left to save!" But a closer look at George's expenses reveals that in reality he has all the money he needs to do what he wants to do.

Each weekday morning George stops by Starbucks for a large espresso coffee and a scone: $6 plus tip. Doesn't seem like much until you add it up: $6 every workday totals $132+ each month. George also carries a cell phone with average charges of $58 per month; makes payments on a pleasure motorcycle at $196 per month; and leases a brand-new car at $269 per month. At home he has the latest high-tech digital connections for both his computer and his big-screen TV and subscribes to a premium TV channel, all totaling $86 per month. George also has five credit cards and carries balances on three of them with minimum monthly payments totaling $225 per month.

Yet poor George has trouble setting aside money in savings. Deep down,

---

You May Be Making
Stupid Mistake #2 If . . .

- you find yourself thinking that, with all your monthly expenses, there just isn't enough money left to save

- a family member has to undergo expensive tests or surgery and you can't readily handle the deductible and copayment without debt

- your car suddenly goes *plooey* and you have to carry the $650 repair bill beyond the thirty-day grace period on your credit card

- you lose your job tomorrow and your present *non-retirement* savings will cover less than three months' regular living expenses while you search for work

- in order to take a much-needed, well-deserved vacation, you have to borrow money or use credit cards to finance it

- you presently have no program in place that automatically shifts money from your paycheck or checking account to a savings plan

- an aging parent needs financial help and you don't have the available cash to come through

---

he knows he should, but life's just too expensive right now. Maybe after his next raise. Or maybe after he pays off his credit cards. Right now, he complains, he barely makes enough to get by, and there's nothing left to save.

What's wrong with this picture?

It's easier to see the problem when you're looking at someone else's finances, isn't it? By convincing himself that he "needs" all of the above in order to endure each day, George has made top priorities of what only a few years ago were considered luxuries—if they were considered at all. (Did you know what a latte was twenty years ago? How about a cell phone or high-speed Internet access?) By deeming such items necessities and regarding them as almost as crucial as housing, food, and clothing, George fritters away at least $966 each month—*that's $11,592 each year*—on unnecessary "necessities" while complaining that "There just isn't anything left to save."

And what happens when a financial emergency comes along? Well, remember, George has those credit cards. He'll whip out a piece of plastic to finance a car repair or a steep medical copayment, which only digs his hole deeper and postpones savings to an even later date.

A Small Priority Shift

Can we help poor George? Can we help him overcome Stupid Mistake #2 and begin setting aside part of his income so he can weather life's fiscal storms and not have to mortgage the future to pay for the present?

You bet we can. And we'll do it without taking away all of his fun, for after all, money is a tool to help us enjoy life. But do you agree that, by making some small shifts in his priorities, George could probably recoup at least one-half of his non-necessity spending? That would enable him to begin setting aside $483 each month in a money market fund—an "emergency reserve" that he could continue building until it reaches the equivalent of three or four months' (truly necessary) living expenses. If that money market fund averages just 4 percent per year, George will build a reserve of more than $12,000 in just two years. In three years it'll grow to $18,442. If he leaves this sum intact and continues to let it grow, it will serve as his "umbrella" for those inevitable rainy days in his future. The result: confidence that he can better handle life's financial emergencies—with cash instead of deeper debt. Peace of mind. Freedom from all those monthly payments. More money to invest more wisely for the future.

Worth the discipline? You bet.

What successful saving comes down to, really, is the daily sense of urgency and priority you assign to it. If disciplined, aggressive saving has been a problem for you, try looking at it this way: If your employer were to suddenly inform you that he had to reduce your salary by $500 per month, you would hustle to find a way to make ends meet. You'd slash frivolities, reduce necessities, and look for sources of supplemental income. Somehow you would adjust your lifestyle in order to "find" the $500 each month you need to make it on your new salary.

Now approach your savings program with the same sense of urgency and priority. You need to steer serious money toward savings, and you can no longer afford to wait until Someday. You need to begin today to build a liquid, accessible contingency reserve that'll be there for you when storm clouds burst.

But when your normal cost of living seems to consume every dollar between paydays, where do you find the money to save? If you find yourself thinking, *I just don't have enough money to save as I should for the future*, don't despair. You may have more money than you think.

Just as we did with George, step back for a moment and contemplate some of your regular expenditures. You just might be amazed at the money that's there for the finding—hundreds, maybe even thousands of dollars each year—that you could easily reprioritize to a systematic savings program for your future. For starters, consider five strategies . . .

1. Adjust a Habit

Let's face it: We all have at least one habit that consumes lots of money. A $4 gourmet coffee each weekday morning adds up to about $88 per month or $1056 per year. A daily $6 fast-food lunch totals $132 each month—$1,584 in a year.

One extra $25 restaurant visit per month totals $300 per year. Adding two $5 desserts to that tab consumes an additional $120 per year.

One additional movie for two each month, with two medium popcorns and two medium soft drinks, can run $26 or more, or $312+ per year.

As you consider the habits of your life, do you see some potential found money? For example, if you were to brown-bag your weekday lunches instead of fast-fooding them, you'd reduce your daily tab from $6 at the nearby BoogieBurger to, say, $1 for your own groceries. You'd "find" approximately $110 each month. That savings alone, redirected to a money market fund averaging just 4 percent, will grow to $7292 over five years. Invest it in a tax-deferred retirement savings program averaging a conservative 8 percent, and in fifteen years it will grow to $38,064.

Do the math on some of your other habits and you'll be amazed at the found money that's there for the saving—and its potential for growth over time.

2. A Penny Saved . . .

I know couples who, by starting early and being consistent, funded most of a child's college education with the following strategy. Likewise, you can use it to help enhance *your* savings for your own long-term needs and dreams.

On almost any given day you come home from work or from a round of errands with loose change in your pocket. Say that on a typical evening you return home with three quarters, a dime, two nickels, and three pennies: 98 cents. Some days you'll have more, some days less, so consider 98 cents an average day.

Place those coins in a jar each evening and watch what happens. At the end of a month your daily 98 cents will total $30 or so. Put each month's savings aside in a money market fund averaging 4 percent and in five years it'll grow to $1989. Invest it in a mutual fund averaging 8 percent, and over the next fifteen years your loose change will grow to $10,381.

And just for the fun of it, what happens if you add just one of the dollar bills in your wallet or purse each evening? In a month your small change is worth around $60. In a money market fund averaging 4 percent your monthly $60 will grow to $3978 in five years. Over fifteen years, invested to average just 8 percent, your found money can grow to $20,762. Small change, big potential!

3. Clean up That Mess

If you're like most American families, you have an extra vehicle (or two) that isn't really necessary but is draining cash for payments, registration, insurance, gas, oil, and repairs. How many hundreds or thousands could you save each year if you were to sell just one of those vehicles? It might mean sharing some rides, but a little planning, communication, and conversation among family members won't hurt a bit.

What about rarely used motorcycles, bikes, RVs, boats, Jet Skis, skis, in-line skates, exercise equipment, tools, or books you'll never read again? Perhaps you've hung on to an old TV set, a CD or tape player, or a CD or video collection. Survey your place for at least three items you could sell for a hundred dollars or more, then place a classified ad and post fliers on the bulletin boards at work. You also may discover that you've accumulated enough stuff to stage a profitable garage sale. Do this once each year, and instead of spending the found money, steer it toward either contingency or long-term savings. Just one $300 lump sum each year, invested at 8 percent over fifteen years, will compound to more than $8145.

4. Enjoy a "Hang around" Vacation

Instead of taking another costly resort vacation, rejuvenate at home this year. Don't tell anyone your plans, turn your phones off, and laze around the house to your heart's content. Sleep in, putter in the garden, paint a landscape, read a novel, take a hike. Play miniature golf. Rent a movie classic. If your vacation would have cost $2500 and you reprioritize that money to savings, your rainy-day fund will receive an immediate, significant boost. Put the $2500 to work in a mutual fund averaging 8 percent over fifteen years, and your found money will grow to $7930.

5. Save Hundreds on Insurance

With some adjustments to your insurance policies you may be able to save a few hundred to a few thousand dollars each year—*without a meaningful decrease in the quality of your coverage.* How?

Consider term life instead of whole life. In the vast majority of cases, you'll receive far greater value for your dollar with a level-premium term-life–insurance policy—much higher coverage, much lower premium. If you feel you'll always want to have some life insurance, then by all means keep whole life as part of your package. But carrying all the coverage you need is much easier on the pocketbook if you buy a level-premium term policy and invest the difference—with the goal of building sufficient assets to be self-insured by the end of the policy term.

Forget life insurance on your children. The chief purpose of life insurance is to replace essential income when a breadwinner dies. Does a child provide income essential to his or her family? Probably not. Therefore, it usually makes little sense to carry life insurance on a child.

Decline credit life and mortgage life insurance. Such specialty insurance is rarely a good value for the consumer, which is exactly why companies pitch it with gusto. You'll save and simplify by accounting for these contingencies in the total face amount of your basic life policy.

Raise your deductibles. Increasing your auto and homeowners deductibles to $500 or $1,000 can cut your premiums by 20 percent.

Maximize discounts. Carry homeowners, auto, and personal-liability policies with the same insurer and receive a multiple-policy discount. Protect your home with deadbolt locks, fire extinguishers, and smoke detectors and receive an additional homeowners-policy discount. Ask about auto insurance discounts for being over fifty-five, having a clean driving record, and equipping your car with air bags, antilock brakes, or antitheft devices.

Let's say you're able to shave $500 a year from your insurance premiums. Redirect this found money to your contingency reserve for an immediate boost. Or put it to work each year at 8 percent, and over fifteen years, your newfound money will grow to $13,576.

Make Savings a Fixed Expense

The above are just some of dozens of areas where, like George, you may find money in your cash flow that you can reprioritize and redirect to savings. Indeed, you probably have more money than you think.

The next challenge is actually making the act of saving happen. Unfortunately, most individuals and couples tend to regard personal savings as an afterthought. We first pay out for all of our monthly expenses, including debt service, then see if there is anything left for savings. But the key to successful saving is to actually reverse this procedure and put Parkinson's Second Law to work in our favor.

Since expenditures are bound to meet (or exceed) income, then the way to make sure we save each month is to *make savings a fixed monthly expense* instead of an afterthought. Instead of saving only when we "have something left to save," we make savings a new high priority, right up there with mortgage payments and groceries. This strategy is called "pay yourself first," and it's the key to diligently setting funds aside to become better prepared for future emergencies, needs, and dreams. (It's also the key to building a financially independent retirement, but we'll focus on that in a later chapter. Today we're talking specifically about being better prepared for the financial surprises that can set us back in the meantime.)

So get aggressive and elbow your way to the front of the line. From this day forward, you are your number one creditor. Personal savings is now one of your most important fixed expenses. From now on, you should steer a predetermined percent of each month's income to savings *before you pay any other bills.*

I know what you're thinking: Paying yourself first goes against human nature. When you have a finite sum of money and a seemingly infinite pile of bills and other spending opportunities, the natural inclination is to pay everyone else first and *then* see if some miraculous aberration leaves you a nickel or two to tuck away for later. But you only have to look at people like George to see the error of this line of thought: How much had he been able to save with the old end-of-the-line approach? *Nada.* For this reason it's vital that, in addition to reprioritizing your spending habits and stepping to the front of the line, you also ensure the act of regular, disciplined savings by making the saving process *automatic.*

Put It in Automatic

Many employers offer a program whereby you can designate a specific amount of your gross income to be deducted from your paycheck and sent directly to a money-market fund on your behalf. Because you do not see the money or hold it in your greedy little hands, you won't even miss it as it goes into your savings. Deposits happen like clockwork, and you'll be amazed at how quickly they add up, assuming you don't deplete your balance every time you have a craving for a piece of new stuff.

If your employer doesn't offer direct deposits to savings, you can still save automatically by arranging an automatic draft from your personal checking account to a money market fund. You can direct the fund to draft biweekly or monthly, depending on which is more convenient for your cash flow. Your only obligation is to be sure you deduct the specified amount from your checking account ledger by the designated day of the draft.

Kathy and I were blessed to learn these principles during the early years of our marriage. We served in a worldwide ministry where the work was abundant but the pay was not, and, although we knew the value of disciplined savings, our savings habits were sporadic at best. It wasn't until we learned about making savings a high-priority fixed expense that we began to grasp the incredible power of the pay-yourself-first principle.

At first we agreed to designate 5 percent of our after-tax income to savings. And at our income level, that was a "reach" for us. I admit that it took some adjusting. But after just a couple of months we realized that we didn't miss the money that was automatically going to savings—our cash flow and budget had reconfigured around our new priority. As the balance in our money market fund grew, we were motivated to keep it going and growing. Soon the pay-yourself-first principle enabled us to purchase our first home. Over time we moved on to other endeavors and our income increased, so we increased the percent of income designated to automatic savings and investment. Like everyone else, we've endured a few financial storms along the way. But Kathy and I can attest to the fact that paying yourself first—*automatically*—has been the key to building and maintaining a rainy-day fund to help weather those storms with minimal damage.

So whether your employer deducts savings from your paycheck or your money market fund deducts it from your checking account, you can send a portion of your earnings to savings *automatically*—before you even have a chance to see it, hold it, or give in to temptation and spend it. Instead of paying everyone else first and ending up with only lint in your pockets, you can truly pay yourself first and build an accessible contingency reserve for the pesky or precarious emergencies in your future.

Aim to build and maintain a reserve equal to at least three months' living expenses. If you work in an industry that tends to experience dramatic swings in employment, you may want to build a reserve that could keep you going at least five or six months.

Where to Save for Those Rainy Days

When a financial emergency comes along, you want to be able to access the needed funds quickly and conveniently. You don't want to have to sell a long-term investment, such as stocks, that may happen to be in a downswing; nor do you want to use funds that would impose taxes and penalties for early withdrawal, as would be the case with a tax-deferred retirement savings plan.

For these reasons, most financial advisers suggest using a *money market fund* as an ideal vehicle for building and maintaining an accessible source of cash for life's inevitable rainy days. It's a type of mutual fund that invests conservatively in an array of short-term vehicles such as certificates of deposit, commercial paper, and U. S. government securities. The better ones will bring you higher returns than a bank savings account while maintaining your need for liquidity and preservation of principal. Unlike regular mutual funds, where your principal fluctuates according to market demand, a money market fund maintains the value of your original investment and pays monthly dividends on the earnings of its portfolio. It is not a guaranteed or insured savings vehicle, but its investments are typically so conservative and short-term that financial experts deem it just as safe, and probably safer, than an insured bank account. If you're in a high tax bracket, you can choose a tax-free fund.

The money market fund you use will come with free check-writing privileges (usually for a minimum amount ranging from $100 to $500) and the option of making automatic deposits on a regular basis. It will require a minimum initial deposit of $500 to $1000 or more (sometimes waived if you sign for the automatic deposit) and minimum subsequent deposits of $50 or more. You won't want to use this account for everyday check writing; maintain your local checking account for that. But your money market fund will serve you well as a convenient, disciplined vehicle for systematic savings.

Money market funds are typically part of a *mutual fund family*, adding extra convenience when you're ready to shift some of your savings into higher-risk, higher-reward vehicles such as stock-and-bond mutual funds. Hundreds of mutual fund families clamor for your savings and investment dollars. Among the best are:

- The Vanguard Group (Prime Reserve Portfolio) 800-662-7447,

- American Century Investments (Prime Money Market) 800-345-2021 or 816-531-5575, and

- Fidelity Investments (Cash Reserves) 800-544-6666.

Customer service representatives at each family will be happy to answer your questions and send you a brochure and application form for the fund. The material will arrive in three to five days. While you wait, determine the amount you will commit to either biweekly or monthly automatic deposits. Try to begin with a minimum of 5 percent of your current take-home pay. If that's too steep under your present circumstances, commit to *something*—$50 per month is better than $0 per month. Eventually you'll be able to increase your automatic savings commitment to 7, 10, 12 percent or more of your after-tax income as you build a cash reserve equaling three to six months' living expenses.

After you receive and read the material for the money market fund, fill out the application. You'll be asked to choose between having monthly dividends mailed to you or reinvested in the fund: choose the *reinvest* option to help your savings compound faster. Mail the application with a check for your initial deposit. Beginning the following month, on the day(s) you have specified, your new money market fund will automatically draft the specified amount from your checking account. All you have to do is leave it alone and watch it grow. You may also want to speed up the growth of your contingency reserve by adding lump sums as they become available, or increasing the amount of the automatic draft to your fund as your income increases.

Your goal is to build, and then maintain, a balance equal to at least three months' regular living expenses. You may want to maintain the equivalent of four, five, or six months' living expenses; the amount is your call and depends on your situation and your comfort zones. The purpose of the rainy-day fund is to serve as an "umbrella" during the sudden downpours of life, to help shelter you and your loved ones from life's urgent needs and expensive surprises so you won't have to take on consumer debt, mortgage your home, or dissipate your retirement savings.

Ready for the Storms

Don't wait till it pours to realize you don't have an umbrella. If you have not yet started a contingency reserve, I want to encourage you to call one of the 800 numbers listed above and get started this month. And if you do have a rainy-day fund but need to build the balance and maintain the balance at a more comfortable level, I hope the motivation and strategies in this chapter will help you do just that.

By making a small shift or two in your spending priorities and redirecting the found money to contingency savings, and by putting yourself at the front of the line by taking advantage of automatic savings programs with money market funds, you can enjoy the peace of mind that comes from knowing that you have a good chunk of cash ready when surprises come. A well-maintained rainy-day fund won't necessarily keep the storms from coming, but it will sure help keep them from washing you away.

Feeding the Monster

*We'll show the world we are prosperous, even if
we have to go broke to do it.*

—WILL ROGERS

It had taken several years for Trent and Julie to realize they needed to talk. Specifically, about their financial situation.

It wasn't that they were in desperate straits. They brought home a good, upper-middle income. Resided with their kids in a nice home in a covetable community. Drove late-model vehicles and enjoyed many of the accoutrements of fine living.

But Julie summed up their frustration in a single sentence: "We aren't in control of our finances; our finances are in control of us."

Trent agreed, with some qualification. "We bring in decent money—we do okay. But money is always tight around our house. We know we need to be saving and investing more, but our monthly nut* just seems to eat it all up."

"And we've talked about how we need to give more," Julie added. "We'd like to give more regularly to our church and to a mission organization that feeds and clothes needy kids around the world. But except

---

* For the uninitiated, *nut* is slang for the total of your monthly financial obligations: housing, food, utilities, vehicle payments, debt service, and whatever else you've committed to that requires regular payments from your wallet to someone else's. (It's a derivative of the Latin term *nutsalotimus*, meaning "What were we thinking? We must have been nuts.")

for a few random gifts here and there, we keep having to put those things off."

As Trent and Julie discussed their situation and we looked at the numbers, it was evident that their income should have provided enough for them to pursue their other financial goals while providing for themselves and their children. I had seen many families do a lot more with much less. Trent had called their monthly financial obligations their "nut." And it was a big nut. At the expense of some other important financial goals, their regular cost of living was consuming almost every dollar they were bringing home.

I offered another term for it. In some financial circles, Trent and Julie's situation is known as "feeding the monster." While we all have basic monthly obligations such as rent or mortgage, utilities, groceries, and car and insurance payments, it is increasingly tempting in our society to continue reaching for more than we presently have. At first, upon graduating or getting married, we may be content to simply "do okay." But before long, "okay" is no longer good enough. An innate human discontent inside all of us combines with advertising, peer pressure, malls, television, the Internet, and even a shaky sense of self to convince us that we really do need—and deserve—more.

It might be another, newer vehicle . . . to make a better impression and to feel better about ourselves.

A bigger, nicer house . . . so we'll be more comfortable and feel more successful.

A cell phone for every family member . . . for convenience, yes, but also so we can feel important by talking while we walk.

A TV with a satellite hookup for every bedroom . . . so neither we nor our kids will feel deprived or have to share.

A handheld computer . . . so we can stay current with appointments, news, and stock quotes and complicate our lives even further.

A "couldn't resist" item from QVC . . . because, although we didn't realize it before we came across the channel, we really can't live without that gizmo.

It's so easy to spin wants into needs. It's almost as if we believe that we are what we own, that we derive and demonstrate our worth by spending and accumulating. But once we step beyond the essential basics to establish any new level of financial obligation for ourselves, we've spawned the monster. He grows larger and more ravenous as we take on one new commitment, then another. Those nurturing the monster eventually find themselves in a vicious feeding cycle: The monster grows huge and hungry. In order to sustain him, we have no choice but to scramble faster, work harder, find more money, take on more consumer debt—in order to continue the care and feeding of the monster. By trying to attain a sense of worth and freedom through spending, we've chained ourselves to Jabba the Hutt.

Feeding the monster is not financial freedom; it's financial bondage. The accumulation of "more" may feel good for a moment, but financing it only keeps us from other things that we know, deep down, are far more important. As Julie put it, we're not in control of our finances; our finances are in control of us.

The Priority Inversion

To help us understand Trent and Julie's mind-set, we could diagram their situation this way:

Figure 1

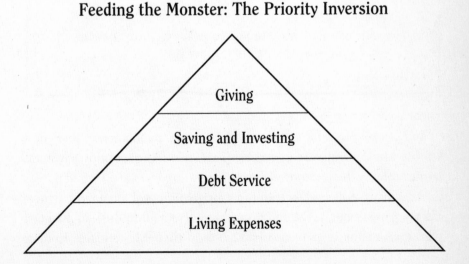

Feeding the Monster: The Priority Inversion

Giving

Saving and Investing

Debt Service

Living Expenses

Their foundational financial priority was meeting their monthly *living expenses*. Their mortgage was nearly five times their annual income. They had three nearly new vehicles for two adult drivers; a speedboat and Jet Skis; a small RV; a riding mower; multiple phone lines and cell phones; and cable TV hookups and PCs for each family member. Considering all the trophies of success to which they had committed themselves, Trent and Julie's monthly "nut" consumed an inordinate percentage of their income.

You May Be Making
Stupid Mistake #3 If . . .

○ your mortgage is more than three times your gross annual income

○ you're not saving or giving what you would like to save or give

○ there's just too much month at the end of your money

○ your garage isn't big enough to hold your vehicles and motorized toys

○ you're paying for multiple phone lines, multiple cell phones, or multiple TV or computer hookups for your family

○ you feel that you are not controlling your finances, but your finances are controlling you

---

And because several of their trophies required financing, their next priority was servicing their *consumer debt*, including monthly payments on the three vehicles and on five different credit cards. In addition to their regular credit card expenditures for gasoline, vehicle maintenance, clothing, meals out, CDs, and furnishings, Trent and Julie had financed Christmas to the tune of nearly $2,200 on their MasterCard (Endless payments at high interest for something your gift recipient won't use more than twice? Priceless.). Combined, their living-expense and consumer debt commitments chained them to one huge, hungry monster.

After feeding their monster, whatever might be left (which wasn't much) went to Trent and Julie's next priority: *saving and investing*. They did contribute small percentages of their gross earnings to their retirement savings plans at work, but they didn't contribute nearly as much as they were entitled to. On rare occasions they managed to tuck away an additional hundred or two in a passbook savings account. But overall, saving and investing were being shoved aside and starved by the ravenous monster.

They had also told me that they wanted to do more *charitable giving*, and to do so more regularly. But, as with their saving and investing, giving was a hit-or-miss proposition. While the need to save, invest, and give weighed heavily on their minds, in practice these were Trent and Julie's least-important priorities.

The insatiable appetite for instant gratification had forced this family into feeding the monster . . . and into hoping for the illusive Someday.

I'm going to go out on a limb here, but I'm confident that it's a strong limb. I'm going to propose that the diagram representing Trent and Julie's situation also represents a good number of other well-intentioned individuals and families in our culture today. It may even represent someone you know . . . quite well.

As you've read about this couple, have you come across anything that reminds you of your own financial picture? You may not be as over-committed to monthly living expenses or debt service as they were, but maybe you *are* feeding a monster of your own—scrambling to keep up with your obligations at the expense of more important things. Perhaps you've recently found yourself wishing that money weren't so tight; felt cornered or consumed by your consumer-debt commitments; realized you aren't saving or sharing what you'd like to be saving or sharing; or caught yourself hoping to "turn things around Someday." Like Trent and Julie, your finances may be in what I call *the priority inversion*—a much-too-common syndrome that causes otherwise smart men and women to live in Someday-type denial while continuing to load up on all the gotta-haves that seem to define contemporary success.

The antidote to the priority inversion is simple, but it is not easy.

Indeed, it may fly in the face of everything you've been doing to keep up with the Joneses or to feel a sense of material progress. It may run counter to some bad habits you might have adopted over the past several years.

But if your finances are anything like Trent and Julie's, the antidote is absolutely critical to finding some fiscal breathing room, to turning your finances around, to meeting your most important and crucial goals, and to freeing yourself from the tyranny of the monster.

It's as simple as committing yourself, mentally, emotionally, and financially, to righting the priority inversion by determining to *put last things first and first things last*—then taking action to make your new priorities the new reality.

Righting the Inversion

As we saw in Chapter 2, the key to successful saving is to pay yourself first. You elbow your way to the front of the line. You send money to your savings program(s) first, before you pay any other bills. This does not mean you pay yourself *more* than you pay your other commitments; it simply means that your savings are of *greater importance*.

Likewise with charitable giving. Trent and Julie really wanted to give more generously to their church and other worthy causes, but because they had chained themselves to the monster, any giving they did was an afterthought.

I personally believe that if there is any financial priority greater than that of saving for the future, it is the act of giving—and not from the dregs of our income, but from the top of our income. Giving is an act of both gratitude and faith: gratitude for the provision and blessings God has given us, and faith that he will continue to do so if we are faithful stewards of those blessings. Giving is sharing from our abundance with those who may be less fortunate or with those who minister to spiritual, emotional, and physical needs all around us. It's the voluntary contributions from people like you and me that sustain all the wonderful ministries and outreaches that help make our world a better place.

But we know how money tends to trickle through our fingers. If we practice giving as something we'll do *if there's money left after everything else*, then we make giving an afterthought. As with saving and investing, the key to successful giving is to right the priority inversion and make giving our top spiritual and financial priority, to write those charitable checks first instead of last.

Making your giving and saving payments from the top of your income will take some adjustment. Write those checks first, and you may have to juggle some of your other commitments or cash flows for a few months. But I can assure you that if you do this faithfully and don't take on additional debt or monthly obligations, your budget will soon adapt to your new priorities. Righting the priority inversion will help your new set of financial priorities look something like this:

Figure 2

Righting the Priority Inversion:
Making the Monster Wait His Turn

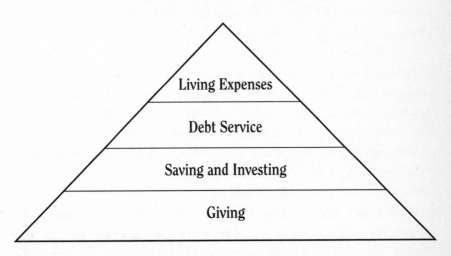

When you right the inversion and put giving, saving, and investing in their rightful places, they will become the first payments you make instead of the last—month in, month out. This ensures that, while you may still be feeding the monster, you're at least going to make him wait until you've first met your highest priorities, after which you will feed him smaller portions. He may growl and snap at you, but you're going to start showing him who's in charge. Gradually, as you whittle down your consumer debt and bring monthly living expenses within reason, you're going to stop feeding him entirely so he'll go away for good.

Keep in mind that we're talking priorities here, not necessarily dollar amounts. Your living expenses will most likely always consume the greatest percentage of your income, but you can find ways to reduce that percentage and free up money to give *now*, save and invest *now*, and eliminate consumer debt *sooner*. Consider all the ways Trent and Julie had encumbered their cash flow. How do you think they could have cut back on living expenses?

Consider their mortgage. At almost five times their annual combined gross income, this family's mortgage was far greater than it should have been. Despite what mortgage lenders tell you, you should try to keep your total mortgage under three times your combined annual gross income. Two-and-a-half times or lower, of course, is even better. By today's lending standards, Trent and Julie could "afford" the higher mortgage (you will almost always *qualify* for more mortgage than you should take on). But their mortgage payments drained their monthly cash flow and prevented them from eliminating debt, saving and investing, and giving.

Now look at all their other obligations. Car payments. Boat and RV payments. Insurance, registration, and maintenance. Multiple phone lines and cell phones. Multiple computer setups. Frequent meals out. If you were Trent or Julie, what steps would you take, starting today, to reduce the size, appetite, and domination of the monster? What would you discontinue? What would you sell? What would you cut back on?

You could do it, couldn't you?

Right the inversion, and you will.

What about debt elimination? Well, Trent and Julie's monster was gorging on consumer debt. But if they first give and save from the top of their income, they'll force the monster to wait his turn. Then, as they work to bring their living expenses within reason, they'll eliminate some consumer-debt obligations (by selling one or more of their expensive toys, for example) while freeing up capital to more aggressively reduce and eliminate their other debt commitments. Eventually, consumer-debt service can go away entirely—providing more capital from each month's income to devote to giving, saving and investing, and, yes, living expenses.

Figure 3

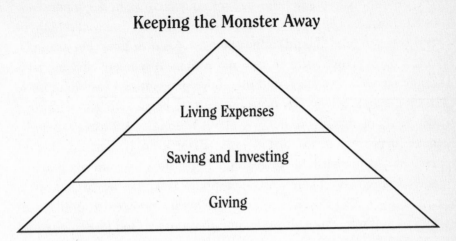

Keeping the Monster Away

Living Expenses

Saving and Investing

Giving

A Spending Plan to Help Keep the Monster Away

No one is going to give, save and invest, eliminate debt, or reduce living expenses for you; it's up to you! To help make it all happen, consider the following guidelines. A and B are what your employer can do for you; C is what you do once the paycheck is in your hands:

A. GROSS MONTHLY INCOME
Less: Deduction for Social Security
Less: Deduction for tax-advantaged retirement savings
(Goal: Contribute maximum allowed by law)
Less: Deduction for medical and flexible spending accounts

= B. TAXABLE MONTHLY INCOME
Less: Federal and state tax withholding
Less: Automatic short-term savings deposit (if available)

= C. NET MONTHLY INCOME ("TAKE-HOME")
1. Giving	10 percent
2. Savings (if not by payroll deduction)	10 percent
3. Debt-service elimination	10 percent
4. Living expenses	70 percent

Keep in mind that this spending plan is simply a guideline and that everyone's situation and priorities are unique. You can begin conservatively or aggressively, you can select some priorities and wait on others, and you can (and should) adjust percentages over time. For example, you may actually desire to *give* more than 10 percent of your take-home pay (C). I've suggested the above percentage as a minimum *to get you started giving first instead of last,* to begin giving something if you've thought you couldn't give at all. You may wish instead to designate 10 percent of taxable income (B) or even 10 percent of gross income (A) to charitable giving and adjust the other priority percentages accordingly. There's an appropriate verse in the Scriptures to guide us: "Each [person] should give what he has decided in his heart to give, not reluctantly or under compulsion, for God loves a cheerful giver" (2 Corinthians 9:7 NIV).

And as you eliminate consumer debt, you can redirect those dollars to any of the other categories. If you don't yet have three to six months' expenses set aside for a major emergency, then building a contingency reserve may be your most urgent priority. In that case, you may need to make smaller contributions to company or personal-retirement programs until you've built that emergency reserve through more aggressive short-term savings. Once that need is met, you can save more aggressively for other short- or medium-term needs so that, in the future, you can put cash on the barrel instead of debt on plastic. You can also increase your commitment to long-term savings until you're able to take full advantage of tax-advantaged retirement programs. It's your call.

A crucial element to this spending plan is that you *learn to live on 70 percent of your take-home pay.* If you cannot, your lifestyle may need the kind of honest self-assessment we've suggested in this chapter. Like Trent and Julie, maybe you have too much house for your income, too many toys in your garage, or too many gizmos in your briefcase. Living on 70 percent of your take-home pay may appear tough at first, but I know you can make the necessary adjustments.

If you've been feeding the monster, I encourage you to make him wait his turn by reordering and living by your priorities. Then, as you work to eliminate consumer debt and get living expenses in line, starve the monster to death and keep him away for good. You'll discover the blessed joy of simplifying your financial life. And perhaps for the first time you'll feel a sense of hope that you can indeed give and save and invest and enjoy life—controlling your finances instead of allowing your finances to control you.

STUPID MISTAKE #4

Believing You Are What You Drive

*The neighbor who has the most expensive car in
the neighborhood has the smallest retirement
account in the neighborhood.*

—JONATHAN POND, *Your Money Matters*

In the market for a new car?"

You tiptoed softly onto the car lot and tried to remain inconspicuous. But as you casually browsed the display vehicles, this grinning salesman suddenly materialized from nowhere, and now he stands just three feet to your left. He has one thing in mind: to keep you on the premises until you buy or lease a car.

He knows the tricks of the trade. He's been trained to get you inside one of those sparkling new vehicles and from there to an uncomfortable straight-backed chair across from his desk in a tiny cubicle where he'll "just run the numbers." His graduate degree is in new-car doublespeak, and it includes a series of car-sales phrases specially formulated to get your name on the dotted line and your money from your pocket to his. If you've ever purchased a vehicle from a dealership, you've heard the buzzwords:

"In the market for a new car?"

"We've got a great deal going on this one."

"This car's a great investment."

"Let's go inside and run the numbers."

"I'll see if I can get my manager to approve this deal."

But because you and I didn't get our graduate degrees in new-car doublespeak, we don't fully comprehend what those buzz phrases *really* mean. As a public service, I'm going to share with you the meanings behind the phrases so you'll be better prepared next time you set foot on a car lot.

12 Stupid Lines People Fall for at a Car Dealership

The following are the twelve stupid things we're most likely to hear from that grinning car salesman, accompanied (in italics) by what the salesman's words really mean:

1. "In the market for a new car?" *You're not getting off this lot for the next three hours.*

2. "We've got a great special going on this one." *We couldn't get rid of it any other way.*

3. "This car's a good investment." *Sure, it'll depreciate $3,000 during the first ten minutes you own it. After that, I'd rather not say.*

4. "These models are disappearing fast." *They're all in the shop out back.*

5. "We'll give you top dollar for your trade-in." *And whatever we allow for your old clunker we'll just hide in your financing so we recoup it in no time.*

6. "Just $19,999." *If you want any extras, like an engine, it'll cost you more.*

7. "Let's go inside and run the numbers." *I'm trained to keep you in my little cubicle until you wear down and sign anything I put in front of you.*

8. "What were you thinking as far as a monthly payment?" *If we tell you the full price of this car, with interest, we'll have to call the paramedics, and they might wheel you away before you sign the papers.*

9. "$175 dealer preparation fee." *This is what we charge you for attaching our logo to the rear bumper.*

10. "$99.99 Premiere Protection Package." *The kid in back, whose dad runs the service department, wipes the dashboard with a rag and Armor All.*

11. "I'll see if I can get my manager to approve this deal." *This is where I disappear for ten minutes to make it look like I'm fighting tooth and nail for you. Then I come back with a sheepish expression, sigh, and tell you I did everything I could but my manager said he can't possibly go this low. He'll come down $150, if you'll settle for recalled tires, but any less than that and you'll drive him out of business and I won't get paid. Do you want my children to go without shoes?*

12. "We'll see if we can get you approved for our payment plan." *You'd have to be dead and buried at least three years for us not to finance you; after all, we're going to clean up on the interest.*

The foregoing public-service announcement is, of course, presented with tongue firmly planted in cheek. I truly respect honest car dealers and their need to make a fair living as they supply the world with needed transportation.

But we now return to our regular programming.

In the last chapter we addressed the Stupid Mistake of "feeding the monster": believing that we are what we own, that we derive and demonstrate our worth by spending and accumulating. We saw how feeding the monster causes millions of good people to embrace a "priority inversion," spending nearly everything they make (and in too many cases, *more than* they make) and procrastinating in giving, saving, investing, and other crucial financial priorities while piling debt upon debt.

Sadly, the monster rarely stops there. It also ravages our finances in another, even more costly way: the manner in which we acquire or lease our forms of transportation. Mark this mistake well, for it is one of life's most enticing, expensive, and oft-repeated financial blunders. Stupid Mistake #4 is believing you are what you drive.

Big Bucks, Temporary Aroma

Granted, we all need reliable—and hopefully attractive—transportation. But for the typical consumer, financing a new car, truck, SUV, motorcycle, or RV is the ultimate monster meal. Today you can easily spend more for an automobile than your mom and dad spent for their house. You may have noticed, however, that the house for which your folks paid $30,000 thirty years ago is now worth $200,000, while the SUV you bought for $30,000 a few years back is now worth only a fraction of that price and will only continue to depreciate in value.

With very rare exceptions such as a classic car, vehicles depreciate extremely quickly—up to one-third of the original price within the first three years of ownership. What *doesn't* depreciate much is the amount you borrowed to buy the car, especially after interest is factored into the equation. High price, interest, and lightning-quick depreciation are why it's not unusual to owe more on your new car after a year or two than the car is actually worth.

Ah, but the lure is powerful, the peer pressure strong—we are what we drive! So we keep paying the big, big bucks for a very, very temporary new-car aroma. When you combine hefty price with rapid depreciation, expensive add-ons, fees, finance charges, and all the other costs glossed over by grinning car salesmen, the way we typically buy a car is one of life's single biggest wastes of good money. We can misspend thousands of dollars on a single car—tens of thousands on multiple vehicles—dollars that can and should be put to far better use in investments that build financial independence for the future.

Is Your Driveway a Car Lot?

On nearly every street of your neighborhood, vehicles spill from overstuffed garages into driveways and even along curbs fronting houses. There are two late-year cars for Mom and Dad. There's a sports utility vehicle for the times Mom and Dad don't want to take one of the cars. There's a pickup truck for tooling about and hauling topsoil on gardening day. And a car for Bobby, age nineteen. A used car, handed down from Bobby to Junior, age seventeen. And one for Missy, who just turned sixteen and gets her solo license soon.

Imagine the monthly payments this family is tied to. The interest. The insurance; registration; gas, oil, and maintenance costs.

Imagine the tension it puts on the family's monthly budget. The strain on their relationships as they constantly wrestle with cash flow and post-pone other financial needs, goals, and dreams.

I am the youngest of four sons. Each of us enjoyed various and sundry activities requiring transportation, and it did become challenging when all of us became old enough to date and to hold after-school or summer jobs. However, at no time before I left for college did my parents own more than one car. We didn't know any better; we just assumed we were fortunate to have a good-looking, reliable car and never felt deprived. We shared plans and shared the car, and, overall, our transportation needs worked out. Life went fairly smoothly for an active family of six. Neither my brothers nor I, to my knowledge, became clock-tower snipers. We really got along quite well, thank you.

My point is, do we *really* need all those cars, trucks, SUVs, motor-cycles, and RVs we think we need?

Are we encouraging our children to have an entitlement mentality— allowing them to assume they each can have their own car as soon as they're of age? Or are we helping them learn to work together as a family?

Does each parent really need a separate car to commute to work? Or could both parents, with just a little more forethought, do just fine with one car between them?

When it comes to transportation, convenience carries a hefty price tag. We're talking payments, interest, gas and oil, batteries, tires, repairs, insur-ance, and registration *for each vehicle.* Plus the time and effort required to administer all of the above. Worth it? Get out your calculator and fig-ure: How many thousands of dollars would you save in the next year if you were to sell one or more of your vehicles and "make do"? How much would you save over the next three years? Five?

Consider one conservative example. Just one of the vehicles over-flowing Bob and Carol's garage requires the following financial support:

Car payment	$2,400 per year ($200 per month)
Insurance	$850 per year
Gas	$1,040 per year ($20 per week)
Oil and lube	$100 per year ($25 per quarter)

Total annual cost for this vehicle alone: $4,390, which averages approximately $365 each month. And this sum does not include any service or repair beyond quarterly oil changes and lubes. If Bob and Carol were to divest their driveway of this one extraneous car and invest the $365 monthly savings over the next five years in a mutual fund averaging 10 percent return, it would mean an additional $28,265 in their nest egg. If they continue investing this monthly "found money" over the next twenty-five years, it'll compound to $484,290. Think about that for just a moment: This single, simple move could result in nearly half a million dollars in just two and a half decades. Could you use another half million twenty-five years from now? (If you don't need it, I run a charitable foundation, the Benson to the Bahamas fund, that will happily accept the half million in your name.) This is just one example of the tremendous financial opportunity you can create simply by getting along with only one less car—and of the huge "opportunity cost" to your nest egg if you insist on keeping that extra vehicle around.

For these reasons, we give the care and feeding of the ravenous vehicle monster its own well-deserved spot among the 12 Stupid Mistakes People Make with Their Money. In an alluring world in which cars, trucks, SUVs, and even motorcycles are confused with status and sex appeal, how can we be financially wise and still drive a good-looking, reliable automobile?

First, Be Courageous

As with many of our Stupid Mistakes, this one is rooted in the internal value system of the consumer. Societal mores, advertisers, peer pressure, and a wobbly self-image all whisper that the vehicle you drive makes a statement about *you*. If you drive something new, popular, and expensive, you're in-touch, vigorous, and successful. But if you drive a vehicle that's more than three or four years old, you're considered to be a bit abnormal, slightly out of touch, and probably struggling with the challenges and finances of daily life.

It's an unfortunate stereotype and one that often masks the rest of the story. Bob and Carol, who drive the sparkling-new sports utility vehicle and have three other cars in their garage and driveway, may in fact be buried up to their nostrils in lease payments and insurance and registration fees, leaving them struggling to meet their other needs. On the other hand, Ted and Alice, who drive a mint-condition four-year-old Honda Accord, may actually be free of car payments and enjoy smaller insurance and registration costs; thus they're freer each month to pursue other interests—including saving and investing for their future. Really, now: Which couple is more likely out of touch, more likely struggling with life's daily challenges?

I'm convinced that saving big money on transportation, and redirecting those thousands toward far more important priorities, begins with the firm conviction that vehicles are intended to help us get to and from in life; they are not life themselves. While it is important that we be good stewards of our transportation, the truth is that what we drive has absolutely nothing to do with our value or self-worth. You are not your possessions, and they are not you. You are not what you own or what you drive. A car is a chunk of metal created by Detroit or Japan or Germany; you are a person created in the image of God.

Once you determine to live by this premise, you'll take on a courageous commitment to disregard the crowd and be your own person. You'll exert a calm confidence, rooted in logic, that a good vehicle is worth waiting for, worth purchasing on your own terms, but *not* worth strapping your cash flow and mortgaging your future. Logic tells you that you need a clean, reliable, and, yes, aesthetically pleasing vehicle that safely gets you where you need to go. Logic tells you that the cost of this vehicle should complement your monthly budget so you can meet your other commitments and save and invest for the future. Logic also assures you that you *don't* need a new, expensive SUV to feel "freedom," you don't need something brand-new every year or two, you don't need what's currently considered "hot," and you don't need high monthly payments at high interest to finance a mere implement that's rapidly depreciating in value.

I know, I know. Waiting is hard because those new cars look so *good*. But you know what? They'll look even better two or three years from now, after someone else has paid the enormous new-car payments, interest, insurance, registration, and depreciation. That's when you'll move in and make a deal for that same sharp-looking vehicle—and save a bundle because you had the courage and confidence to bide your time.

You May Be Making
Stupid Mistake #4 If . . .

○ you own or lease more than one vehicle per adult family member

○ you own a vehicle of any type that is not used at least twice each week for necessary transportation

○ your annual vehicle payments total more than 5 percent of your annual gross income

○ you insist on buying or leasing a brand-new vehicle

○ you step onto a car lot to browse without knowing the make, model, and year of the vehicle you want as well as its current Edmund's or Kelley Blue Book price

---

The Buy-or-Lease Dilemma

When it's time to make your move, should you buy or lease? Leases have grown in popularity because they make it easier to go home with more car. Not necessarily wiser, but easier. With a lease, the down payment is usually smaller and monthly payments are usually lower than with a car loan. However, you still need to come up with a down payment and a security deposit, plus the requisite insurance and registration. And there are subtle costs to a lease that, in the long run, make leasing less attractive and more expensive than buying. Here are some examples:

- At the end of a lease (anywhere from twenty-four to sixty months), you can turn the car in, but you then are without a car and will need to acquire another. Lease another, and you start the clock all over again: down payment, security deposit, new-car registration, new-car insurance premiums. When you buy a car and pay it off, you own it free and clear and can drive it as long as you like—ten, fifteen years, or more—with only upkeep to think about.

Registration fees and insurance premiums get smaller the longer you have the car.

- Leases usually come with mileage limits of 12,000 to 15,000 per year; exceed the limit, and you'll pay a hearty per-mile premium for each additional mile.

- When you lease a car, the lessor determines your minimum insurance coverages. Try to economize on coverages, and you'll receive a nastygram advising that you are hereby required to increase your coverage to a specified minimum. Again, the lessor holds the power.

- A lease can dock you for "excessive wear and tear," a term subject to the interpretation of the leaseholder. Could be nothing, could be enormous. But it does give the lessor an uncomfortable level of power over you.

- At the end of the lease, you can purchase the car for the "residual"— the difference between the original total lease price and what you've paid in. Quite often, especially on longer leases, the residual is significantly higher than the actual book value of the car due to our friend, depreciation.

So while a lease can feel like a short-term cash-flow solution, its drawbacks can make it a poorer use of money in the long run. In general, you'll do better if you buy instead of lease. Especially if you . . .

Buy "Almost New"

Cars depreciate so rapidly in their first two to three years that it makes a lot of sense to look for a well-maintained vehicle that's two to three years old. With a little patience, you can find a make and model you like that is properly maintained inside and out and almost ding-free. Have a trustworthy mechanic give the car a thorough physical before you buy. If it checks out mechanically and you purchase the vehicle, you may even want to drop a few hundred more to make any windshield pits or body dings disappear.

Remember, too, that the price of registration and insurance goes down as a vehicle ages. By choosing an almost-new car over a brand-new one, you'll save hundreds of dollars per year in these expenses alone.

But a good two- or three-year-old car is still a major expense, and whether you're buying from a dealer or private source, it's a Stupid Mistake to accept the initial asking price before doing some homework. Once you spot a pre-owned car that appeals to you, take down the key details—make, model, year, engine size—then check its estimated value in *Edmund's Used Car Prices*, a book that's updated annually (free estimates at www.edmunds.com) or at the Kelley Blue Book Web site (www.kbb.com). The estimated value you find in your research should be your ceiling. Then begin your search by checking www.autotrader.com for the pre-owned make, model, and year you're looking for. Check your local classifieds as well as the Web sites of local dealers. Once you find a promising vehicle, and with your top price clearly in mind, offer a price significantly below that sum and wait calmly for the seller's response. If he resists or counterproposes, consider his position for a moment; then inch your offer upward slightly until you reach a win-win agreement. Be prepared to courteously walk away if he holds to a price greater than your research justifies.

If researching, searching, and haggling don't appeal to you, you may want to engage a car-buying service. You'll pay a fee, but you'll avoid the time-consuming hassle with the grinning salesperson at the car dealership. Check your yellow pages for local services or the American Automobile Association's car-buying service (www.aaa.com).

If at All Possible, Pay Cash

Should you borrow to pay for the purchase of a car? I like the way Eric Tyson, author of the best-selling *Personal Finance for Dummies*, lays it on the line:

> You should avoid borrowing money for consumption purchases, especially for items that depreciate in value like cars. . . . If you lack sufficient cash to buy a new car, I say "DON'T BUY A NEW CAR!" Ninety percent of the world's population can't even afford a car, let alone a new one! Buy a car that you can afford—namely not a new one. Don't fall for the new-car buying

rationalization that says that buying a used car means lots of maintenance, repair expenses, and problems. If you do your homework and buy a good used car, you can have the best of both worlds. A good used car costs less to buy and should cost you less to operate thanks to lower insurance costs.

Amen, Eric. Borrowing for depreciating or consumable items is one of life's Stupid Mistakes. And if you're implementing the savings strategies discussed in this book, I'm confident you'll reach a point in the near future at which you can indeed pay cash for your next car and free up hundreds of dollars each month for other priorities.

Okay, If You Must Finance . . .

But in the meantime, I realize it's tough out there. If you absolutely *must* borrow to purchase a car, please do so only after you

- drive the hardest bargain you can and pay no more than the Blue Book value;
- shop aggressively (at least three sources) for the best financing;
- promise to finance for no more than thirty-six months (if you can't pay up in thirty-six months, you can't afford the car)—less time if at all possible;
- commit to continue making car payments after the loan is paid off—payments to *yourself*. That's right, keep 'em flowing to your savings so that next time you can pay cash on the barrel;
- commit to driving the car till it dies. Own it free and clear, keep it serviced, and treat it like one of the family until it absolutely will go no farther. This is the best way to make the high cost of car ownership somewhat worthwhile. Most number-crunchers agree: *The least-expensive car is the one you already own.*

Insure Wisely

It pays to shop for car insurance. Rates constantly change, and you'll find that the same coverage can differ among carriers by $200 to $500 per year.

You want to carry *liability* coverage of at least $100,000 per person and $300,000 per occurrence. In our sue-happy culture, it's smart to supplement this liability coverage with a separate *excess liability (umbrella)* policy, a relatively inexpensive plan that covers you for $1,000,000 or more in the event of a lawsuit.

To keep premium costs down, use the highest deductibles you're comfortable with on both *collision* (damage arising from bumping into someone or someone bumping into you) and *comprehensive* (damage from other causes such as hail or vandalism). At minimum, take a $500 deductible on each; $1,000 will save you more if you have built an adequate savings reserve to cover such contingencies. Consider dropping these coverages altogether as your car ages—why continue paying high premiums to cover damage when insurance companies won't pay more than the book value of your car?

Be sure you're taking advantage of good-driver discounts, multiple-car discounts, multiple-policy discounts (if you insure home, auto, and excess liability with the same company), antitheft-device discounts, and safety-feature discounts (air bags, antilock brakes). Forget riders such as towing and car-rental reimbursement; you'll do better on those as part of a AAA membership without the hassle of filing a claim.

The Wiser Path

You can save thousands of dollars in transportation costs just by doing your homework, shopping smarter, and choosing the wiser path instead of following the crowd. A vehicle is an expense, not an investment. Regard it accordingly, stay strong and courageous in the face of advertising and societal pressure, and you'll be able to drive an attractive, reliable vehicle while keeping your expenses as low as possible. By investing those savings instead of smoking them in your exhaust pipe, your nest egg can be tens of thousands of dollars richer down the road.

Borrowing Trouble

If the shoe fits, charge it.

It happens nearly every week, doesn't it?

You get home from a tough day's work, and it's waiting for you, right there in your mailbox. Another friendly letter that begins something like this:

Dear Mr. and Mrs. Smith:

Because of your outstanding credit history, you are already PRE-QUALIFIED to enjoy the prestige and convenience of owning your very own platinum Bank of Perpetual Payments credit card . . .

The letter is accompanied by a slick brochure picturing a carefree couple strolling along an exotic beach. It extols the peace of mind you'll have once that platinum credit card is in your wallet: Escape the rat race. Take that well-deserved vacation. Fix up your house. Consolidate your debts. Purchase that new wardrobe or buy that new entertainment system.

Freedom!

Prestige!

Your chance to get ahead!

Why, this nice bank will even send you a check for your first $2,500, conveniently charged to your new card, to tide you over until your personally engraved platinum card arrives. And that's just for starters—you can have more credit if you want it by simply requesting a higher amount on the handy "Make Your Dreams Come True" application form, and receive more cash advances whenever you want, at thousands of convenient locations around the world.

By now you're supposed to be so excited about all the things you can do with your very own platinum credit card that you'll sign right up, totally ignoring the hidden message of the mailing. What the Bank of Perpetual Payments doesn't make clear (but *does* include, for legal reasons, in tiny print on the back of the handy "Make Your Dreams Come True" application form) is that it expects you to pay back all this money it's giving you, and at interest rates that would shame a loan shark. Another thing it doesn't mention is that it hopes you will pay your debt back v-e-r-y s-l-o-w-l-y so it can keep compounding that high interest into your debt balance. This is how the bank makes its big bucks. And how you lose yours.

"Let's Just Charge It"

One couple, Michael and Cynthia, never asked for their first credit cards. Shortly after they were married, offers of four cards showed up in their mailbox.

Michael and Cynthia were well educated, and together they brought home a good income. "We used credit cards for whatever caught our fancy," Cynthia recalls. They drew frequent cash advances and made only minimum payments. Whenever they reached the credit limit on one card, they started spending on another.

Within five years this well-meaning couple owed more than $32,000 on sixty-three credit cards. With their payments running at least six weeks late, all those nice banks sent more letters—only now the letters had a nasty tone and demanded payment. Michael and Cynthia report that the stress of being so far in debt nearly tore them apart.

This couple's consumer-debt burden was far above the national average, but their story is a vivid illustration of how easily individuals and couples slip into the "let's just charge it" trap. Typically, we do not acquire credit cards with the intention of running them up into the stratosphere.

The usual rationale for the first card or two is that "it'll be good to have for emergencies."

But then emergencies happen. Like the "emergency" dinner out or the "emergency" vacation. Wander through a mall with a credit card, and practically any item can become an emergency. Besides, you'll pay off the full amount when the statement arrives, right?

Right. Before that moment of truth comes, another pressing need has surfaced—the VCR with thirty-year advance programming from TV's shopping channel. So you send just the minimum payment to your credit card company for now. And during the next month, more emergencies become just too important to pass up. The balance grows. So does the interest. You lose; the bank wins.

The Two Faces of Credit

Credit can be a tremendous asset to individuals and families who respect it for what it is: a tool to help them acquire appreciating assets such as a home, investment real estate, or a promising business. Credit can tide you over in a genuine emergency, such as a needed medical procedure or getting stranded miles from home. In business, a strong line of credit is essential for capital investment and as a buffer against the inevitable ups and downs of cash flow.

In addition, a reality of our society is that good credit is necessary for much of the routine business of life. Lenders usually want to see a positive credit history before they loan money for a new home, automobile, college education, or business venture. A valid credit card is almost mandatory for renting a car or staying in a hotel. And properly utilized, credit can be a helpful, effective cash-flow management tool for both individuals and businesses.

But I emphasize *properly utilized*. Like most good things in life, credit is meant to be used wisely, as a very temporary cash-flow bridge until the bill comes due. Where many of us get into trouble is in using charge cards and credit cards for depreciating or perishable items, then carrying the balances from one month to the next as interest builds. The average American family holds a credit card debt of more than $8,000 on at least eight cards. And this does not include notes owed on cars, trucks, sports utility vehicles, or expensive toys such as RVs, campers, or all-terrain vehicles.

I remember a young couple who talked with me following a financial planning seminar. Married just seven months, they had accumulated debts of more than $17,000 on several credit cards for furniture, clothing, and appliances. Interest rates for these purchases averaged more than 19 percent annually, obligating them to approximately $3,200 per year in interest payments alone. With monthly take-home pay of $2,200 and minimum monthly credit card payments totaling $1,200, they were hard-pressed to pay their rent, purchase food, and provide for the other necessities of life. Savings and investment, of course, were out of the picture entirely.

Why Consumer Debt Doesn't Make Sense

But the friendly mailings proclaim, "Using our card is so *easy*. So *convenient*." Sure, consumer credit may be easy and convenient to use, but what the sales pitch does not tell you is that once you've run up your credit card balance, consumer debt is neither easy nor convenient. In fact, you're only borrowing trouble.

First, *borrowing on depreciating or consumable items pits the power of compounding against you.* When you charge purchases of appliances, clothing, tools, computers, meals out, vacations—anything that does not *appreciate in value* over time—you're robbing your future to pay for your past. You will pay 16, 18, 20 percent interest, sometimes spreading the payback over several years, while the item rapidly decreases in value. In the case of consumable goods, the depreciation is instantaneous—yet you're stuck paying for them over the course of several months.

Second, *servicing your debt prevents you from doing more positive things with your money, such as saving and investing for future needs and dreams.* When you carry consumer debt, your monthly income can become so tied up paying for depreciating or perished items that you are unable to build your own emergency reserve, save for planned expenditures, invest for your retirement years, or give to your church or favorite charity. To state it succinctly, *consumer debt consumes* . . . your income, your cash flow, your flexibility, your future.

Scott, for example, is making payments totaling $260 each month on his credit card balances. I'd like to tell you that he's paying those balances down, but I can't, because he's not. Instead, Scott keeps feeding the monster by charging as much as or more than he's paying down each month. Paying $260 every month in debt service is costing Scott big-time—and not just in depleted monthly cash flow.

Scott's biggest blunder is what we call "opportunity cost"—a bigger, better opportunity he's missing because of his monthly debt obligation. If he were free of that monthly $260 debt service and instead added it to his 401(k) or IRA averaging 8 percent per year, in twenty years Scott would have an additional $153,145 in his retirement savings. Big opportunity! But instead of putting his hard-earned money to work for his future, he's shelling it out to creditors to use for *their* futures. Opportunity lost!

Third, *borrowing places you at a relational disadvantage as well as a financial one.* The ancient proverb speaks wisely for today: "The rich rule over the poor, *and the borrower is servant to the lender*" (Proverbs 22:7 NIV, emphasis added). When you owe money, the lender calls the shots. He dictates minimum payments, interest charges, and due dates. He makes the profit; you take the loss. If the lender is someone you know personally, you may experience a degree of discomfort whenever you're in the same room, working in the same building, attending the same church, or residing in the same town. The obligation constantly hovers between you. Being "servant to the lender" is no picnic, and it's definitely not financial freedom.

The harsh truth is that consumer debt does not get you ahead; it holds you back. Purveyors of credit cards won't tell you this. Neither will the department stores, TV shopping channels and infomercials, or Web sites for purchasing stuff on the Internet (www.poorhouse.com). All they want you to do is buy now and (they hope) pay forever—making only minimum payments so they can profit handsomely from all the interest that accrues on your balance.

In his play *A Doll's House,* Henrik Ibsen wrote, "There can be no freedom or beauty about a home life that depends on borrowing or debt." It's true! Being ensnared in consumer debt is one of the "easiest, most convenient" Stupid Mistakes people make, and one of the primary reasons they fail to achieve financial freedom. They're so busy paying for their past that they have little to set aside for their future.

Are You Borrowing Trouble?

Where do you stand when it comes to consumer debt—on solid ground or in quicksand? Take a few quiet moments to honestly answer the following questions:

- *Do my consumer debts total more than 5 percent of my gross income?* Get out your most recent credit card and installment-card statements, car-payment information, and any other documents showing what you presently owe for items or expenses that have been consumed (such as vacations, food, and gasoline) or are depreciating in value (everything other than real-estate mortgages or investment in a growing business).

  If you have taken out a home-equity loan or carry a balance on a home-equity line of credit, do not include expenditures you may have made from these sources to increase the basis (assessed value) of your home, such as a finished basement, a permanent addition, trees, or landscaping. Such expenditures are usually not considered consumer debt because, more likely than not, they are invested in an *appreciating* asset. However, if you have made the common mistake of using a home-equity loan or line of credit for a consumable or depreciating item, be sure to include the total of those expenditures in this calculation of your total consumer debt.

  With all those statements stacked neatly in front of you, add all your current balances. The sum is your *total consumer debt*. Hopefully, your calculator display has enough digits to show this sum.

  Now divide your total consumer debt by your annual gross income. If the result is more than 5 percent, consumer debt is playing far too big a role in your financial life. For all the reasons we've discussed, you want to bring your consumer debt down to zero and keep it there.

- *Do I consistently pay only the minimum amount due each month on installment or credit card purchases?* Remember, your paying only the minimum amounts due is how creditors make money. *Your* money. It's in *their* best interest that you pay them as little as possible for as long as possible. They want the awesome power of compounding interest to work in *their* favor, not yours. Anytime you let interest accrue on consumer debt by not paying in full, you are allowing compound interest to work against you—at the profit of someone else.

- *Do I tend to add more expenses to an account than I can pay off at the end of the same month?* If you add $75 in charges this month and make a payment of only $50, you've carried $25 over into next month on top of your existing balance. That carryover will accrue interest, making your balance even bigger. Continue this from month to month, and you have the proverbial snowball effect.

- *Do I find I'm charging consumable or depreciating items that were formerly purchased with cash?* Meals out, vacations, gasoline, oil-and-lube services, clothing, or anything else that is consumed or that depreciates in value should be paid with cash. Do not put such items on credit unless you have the firm resolve and discipline to pay these charges *in full* when the statement arrives. Most people do not, unless the sum of such purchases is very low. But why tempt yourself? Just two or three of these modest expenditures can add up.

- *Do I lack a sense of inner peace about my consumer-debt situation?* If you've been fighting that "gotta get out of debt" feeling or have ever had to say, "Maybe when I get out of debt . . ." or have experienced worry over your financial obligations, you are experiencing symptoms of financial bondage instead of financial freedom. Financial freedom means freedom from worry and obligation, a peace of mind that results from wisely keeping your spending and consumer debt under control. If you've felt a lack of peace about your debt picture, it's time to get tough with yourself and take the necessary steps to turn your situation around.

- *Have I received any late-payment penalties or letters or phone calls about late payments?* Late payments are a sure sign that you're having to juggle your finances due to excessive commitments.

- *Am I unable to consistently put at least 10 percent of my gross earnings toward long-term savings and investment?* A long-term savings program of at least 10 percent of your gross income is a fundamental secret of financial freedom. Saving less than that is going to prevent you from reaching your goals. If servicing consumer debt forces you to cheat your savings program, your consumer debt is too high.

If you answered "yes" to any of these questions, it's possible you have allowed the "buy now, pay forever" syndrome to mire you in consumer debt. If so, you're making your present financial life much tougher than necessary. It's no fun being "servant to the lender." You're *definitely* compromising your financial future by using today's dollars to pay for things that happened weeks, months, or years ago. Perhaps most seriously, your finances may actually be in jeopardy without a swift and sure midcourse correction.

But please don't despair—this doesn't mean you're a bad person. You're a good person who simply encountered a bad streak of luck or made a bad decision or two. People in far worse shape have become debt-free, and so can you.

And it's going to feel so good.

The Blessings of Being Debt-Free

When you stop borrowing trouble, here's how your financial life will turn around.

First, *you're going to be in control of your cash flow.* When you no longer have to service those debilitating monthly debt payments, you have more money to enjoy life, handle emergencies, give to your church or favorite charity, build your savings reserve, and invest for future dreams.

Second, *you'll stop the drain of compound interest working against you and get it working* for *you.* Instead of paying 16, 18, 20 percent on the money you owe, you can earn 4 to 12 percent (sometimes more) on those funds as you redirect them toward savings and investments. Eliminate the debt payments, add the earnings, and in effect you'll be earning 20 to 32 percent on those dollars!

Third, *you will dramatically speed up your journey toward financial independence.* An average monthly credit card payment of $75 over the next twenty-five years robs you of $22,500 you could be saving and investing.

However, with that debt paid off, you can contribute that $75 to tax-deferred investments where, at 10 percent, it can grow to more than $99,500 over the same twenty-five years. This is why you don't want to pay today for yesterday's indulgences—or pay tomorrow for today's. Becoming debt-free will free up those debt-servicing dollars and turn them into you-servicing dollars.

You May Be Making Stupid Mistake #5 If . . .

o you carry more than one credit card in your wallet

o you pay by credit card for anything that's perishable or depreciates in value

o you cannot pay each card's balance *in full* at the end of this month and every month

o your monthly debt service is keeping you from maxing your 401(k) or building your rainy-day fund

o you or your spouse feels a lack if inner peace about your debt load

Fourth, *you will feel financially free.* This is perhaps the greatest benefit of all. No longer will you feel like an oppressed "slave to the lender," making endless payments on depreciating or already-consumed purchases. You'll enjoy the peace of mind that comes from staying current and paying as you go—and peace of mind is one of the best returns on investment you'll ever have.

How to Stop Borrowing Trouble

Today you're going to launch a simple but powerful, nine-step strategy to attain freedom from consumer debt. And believe me, you'll begin enjoying the benefits almost immediately.

Step 1: Commit to becoming debt-free—for good.

Decide now, boldly and irrevocably, that you will take on absolutely no more credit card debt. From this moment forward, you will cease robbing your future to pay for your past. You will operate strictly on a cash-only, pay-as-you-go basis. In other words, if the cash is not in your wallet or checking account, you will not spend it.

No more debt.

If You're in over Your Head

It's possible that you find yourself so mired in debt that you haven't been able to meet even the minimum monthly obligations. If you've recently skipped payments, been penalized for paying late, or had creditors teepeeing your house, run—don't walk—to seek help from a nonprofit credit-counseling service. For example, Consumer Credit Counseling Service (800-388-2227) has hundreds of offices throughout the country. The cost of its services is free or minimal, and it will work with you and your creditors on a payback schedule you can handle. (Caution: Think twice before using a for-profit credit counselor; after paying the fee, you could be in a deeper hole than before.)

As you seek to live by this commitment, keep that mantra at the forefront of your mind. When temptation comes—and it will—say it to yourself: *No more debt.* If you feel you need something now but would have to put it on credit, *No more debt.* If you can't afford to pay cash today, you can't afford to pay with compounded interest tomorrow.

No more debt. It's your new resolution, your new way of life. You can do it, and you'll be glad you did.

Step 2: Reduce your card collection to one card.

Today—*right now*—you can gain a huge degree of control over your spending by reducing your number of credit cards to one.

I realize that this step may seem melodramatic, but if you can summon the courage to take it and live by it, you'll be rewarded many times over. Here's what to do:

First, pull every credit card from your wallet: Visa, MasterCard, Discover, You-Name-It. Don't forget department-store cards, chain-store cards, oil-company cards—any card that will charge interest if you carry a balance with it.

Second, select the no-annual-fee Visa, MasterCard, or Discover card with the lowest interest rate. Set this card aside.

Third, find the sharpest pair of scissors you own. Take each card from the pile, insert it between the scissors, and *slice away.* I know, it sounds drastic. Even painful. Like excising cancerous growths from your body, you're excising harmful growths from your financial life. It may hurt a bit, but you know you must do it to keep those growths from metastasizing. You're going to halt the sickness in its tracks and get healthy again.

Let me assure you, you are doing the smart thing. Contrary to what your world tells you, *you do not need all these cards.* You are not what you can buy; you are not what you drive; and you are not the number of credit cards you own. You're going to get along just fine without all these cards. You're going to pay off your balances and close these accounts, never to be pulled down by them again. You're going to experience the freedom of being debt-free. Instead of serving your lender, your money is going to serve you.

Strange as it may seem, shredding your card collection is among the most pivotal steps you can take to improve your financial picture.

Step 3: Remove temptation: Keep your surviving credit card out of your wallet.

Hopefully you are now looking at (1) one no-fee, low-interest credit card and (2) one pile of plastic shards. Do not entertain second thoughts, gasping, "What have I done?" as you dash for a bottle of Elmer's glue. You have definitely done the right thing. *No more debt. You do not need those shredded cards.*

You now have one credit card. This is going to serve as your one card to keep in reserve for a genuine emergency. But it is no longer a license to spend. So the next strategy is to *make your one low-interest credit card more difficult to access.* Instead of putting this card back in your wallet, hide it in a place so inconvenient that you'll be forced to pause and think seriously before you use it. You might hide it in a cupboard or drawer or keep it in a safe-deposit box at your bank. Accessible, but not *too* accessible. Some people I know have even frozen their credit cards in water-filled milk cartons, knowing that waiting for the thaw is likely to give them enough time to settle down and reconsider a tempting credit card expenditure.

Step 4: Carry a debit card instead of a credit card.

Most likely your bank offers either a Visa or MasterCard *debit card,* which looks and acts much the same as a credit card but with one wonderful difference: If you pay with a debit card, the expense is automatically deducted from your checking account. Thus it does not accrue interest and does not add to your consumer debt.

Some banks charge an annual fee for a debit card, but consider this expense an investment in personal discipline; the fee pales in comparison to the high interest you'd pay on credit card balances. On the upside, a debit card can get you through most of the financial surprises that come your way. You can keep the credit card safely ensconced because most establishments will honor your debit card just as they do a credit card. If necessary, you can later transfer funds from your contingency savings to your checking account to cover the emergency expense.

Do not, however, use a debit card to excuse excess spending. The natural result will be too much month at the end of the money. Consider it a convenience meant only to bridge those occasions when you don't have sufficient cash in your wallet for a normal expense. Just be certain that (1) you have enough funds in your checking account to cover the expense, (2) it's an expense your spending plan already calls for, and, most important, (3) you deduct the expense from your checking ledger immediately so it doesn't surprise you when the statement arrives.

Step 5: Prioritize your creditors.

List names, phone numbers, the balance owed on each account, the interest rate you're paying, the minimum required payment, and your current monthly payment. Then look over your list and determine whom you'd like to pay off first, second, third, and so on.

You have three options here. You may wish to pay off the smallest debts first in order to give yourself an emotional boost and sense of accomplishment. Or you may wish to prioritize your creditors from "most urgent" to "least urgent"—perhaps you've received nastygrams from creditors you've been slow in paying, and you'd like to rebuild your honor with them by repaying them more aggressively than the others. Another option is to rank your creditors from the "most expensive" to the "least expensive" by analyzing which are costing you the most in monthly interest and eliminating the most costly debts first.

Though good arguments can be made for all three, I've found that people who have borrowed trouble tend to do best when they target their smallest balances first. Paying off a creditor and crossing him off the list provides a big psychological boost and makes you even more determined to continue the process.

When you've made your decisions, take a clean sheet of paper and list your creditors again, this time according to payment priority.

Step 6: Assign a monthly payment to each creditor.

You're going to pick off your creditors one at a time while keeping the others happy. All creditors except your top priority will receive their minimum monthly payment until it's their turn to move to the top. Meanwhile, you're going to send as much as you can every month to your top-priority creditor—*the minimum payment plus at least $50.* If you can possibly send $75, $100, or more above the minimum, do it.

Be diligent about making each monthly payment on time. True, you've made confetti of all your credit cards except one, but those accounts are still active and open. You're still receiving monthly statements from each creditor, and they'll keep on coming until you've paid them in full. So never allow a payment to be late, and never make a creditor call you. No matter how deep the hole, you will climb out of it responsibly and with integrity. You'll demonstrate good faith and feel much better about yourself when you're diligent with every payment.

Step 7: Apply some found money.

You can slice some girth from your debt load with a couple of big lump-sum payments, courtesy of any found money that comes along.

Your first source of found money, of course, is personal savings. Many financial experts rightly point out that it makes little sense to keep money in a savings account earning 3 to 5 percent interest while carrying consumer debt at 18 percent. Pay off the consumer debt ASAP and, by doing so, you will virtually earn a guaranteed 18 percent on your investment.

However, there's another important side to this argument. Remember, you've committed to *no more debt*. What happens if, as you focus diligently on paying off your debts, a big emergency enters your life? For this reason I like to see people maintain a minimum of $1,000 in their contingency reserves even while working off their consumer debt. If you have *more than $1,000* in savings, you might take between one-fourth and one-half of the extra and make a lump-sum payment against your top-priority debts.

As we saw in Chapter 2, you probably have other sources of found money as well. Now's an excellent time to put those dollars to work. For example, if you were to clean house, basement, and garage and hold a yard sale next weekend, you may earn several hundred dollars to apply to your top-priority debts. The "penny saved" strategy by itself could locate an immediate $50 or $60, plus another $30 or so every month that you can devote to debt elimination.

Found money also comes along in the form of tax refunds, bonuses or raises at work, and even anticipated expenses that you budgeted for but that turn out to be unnecessary. As long as you're in debt-payoff mode, use any found money to make additional payments to your top-priority creditor.

With found money, you may find that you can completely eliminate a debt or two. At the very least, your found money can help you make a significant dent. The idea is to make the minimum payment, on time, to every other creditor on your list *while you diligently send as much as possible to your top priority.*

Step 8: Once an account is paid off, formally close the account.

Once you've paid off an account, your next joyous act is to formally close the account so that neither you nor anyone else can use it again. You've already shredded the piece of plastic that got you in trouble in the first place; now, to ensure that the account is closed properly, *write* the credit card company and request that it (1) close your account and (2) confirm *in writing* that it has done so *at your request.* Keep the written confirmation on file so that, if necessary, you can verify that the account was closed at your behest instead of the credit card company's.

Step 9: Knock off the other creditors, one by one.

You're making progress, but you aren't there yet. As you eliminate one top-priority debt and close the account, move your next creditor to the top of the list and shower him with the same number of dollars you had been paying your first creditor: the minimum monthly payment, *plus $50, $75, $100, or more.* Continue looking for additional found money, both monthly and lump sum, to apply to your top-priority debt. Meanwhile, stay faithful with your other creditors by paying them their minimum payments on time. Stay faithful to yourself by fiercely resisting any new credit spending while you're working so hard to become debt-free.

Beware of More Convenient
Ways to Borrow Trouble

I predict that you will continue to receive warm, fuzzy letters from the Bank of Perpetual Payments. You will see tempting signs as you enter department stores: *Apply Now for Instant Credit and Receive 10% Off Today's Purchases!* And, as you draw closer to paying off a balance, the credit card companies will inform you that because you're such a stellar customer, they're going to do you a big favor and increase your credit limit.

Our modern financial world offers more and more easy ways to get yourself seriously sucked back into debt. They include (but are not limited to):

Should You Use Home-Equity, Debt-Consolidation, or 401(k) Loans to Pay Off Consumer Debt?

Many financial publications are quick to recommend that you pay off high-interest credit card debt with lower-interest home-equity loans, debt-consolidation loans, even loans against your 401(k). Good idea? From a strictly-by-the-numbers perspective, such moves might make sense by trading high-interest debt for lower-interest debt. But there are more important factors to consider.

As stated earlier, a house is usually an appreciating asset; thus, it generally isn't wise to use home equity to pay off debt for depreciating or consumable items. In addition, using your home as collateral against consumer debt only places the future of your home in the hands of more creditors. Ideally, if you tap your home equity at all, it should be for appreciating endeavors such as finishing a basement or some other improvement that increases your home's resale value.

- With these caveats in mind, consider using home equity to expunge consumer debt only if you can exercise the discipline to make it a one-time, benchmark event in your journey to financial freedom. In other words, borrow only the amount you need to completely eliminate your consumer debts once and for all. (Resist every temptation to add an extra $5,000 for a trip to Hawaii.) Then, with consumer debts completely paid, swear on the graves of your dear, departed ancestors that you will never, ever build up consumer debt again or deplete home equity to service it.

The advantages of using home equity in this way are (1) all your debts are consolidated into one, (2) your interest rate will probably be lower, and (3) the interest you pay will most likely be tax-deductible. But if you cannot swear on the grave of your dear, departed ancestors, don't take out the loan.

- Avoid debt-consolidation loans altogether. These are favorites of the financial-services industry because, while purporting to decrease your monthly minimum payment, they do so by stretching your payments out forever. Some creditors require minimum monthly payments as low as 1.7 percent of your total balance. Factor in the interest, and at this rate you'll be paying for thirty years or more. Good for the lender, bad for you. Follow your nine-step program to do your own consolidating.

- A loan against your 401(k)? Don't ever go there. Plug your ears to all the hype about how you can borrow against a 401(k) or 403(b); the opportunity cost and potential penalties are overwhelming. Whatever your debt situation, consider these tax-advantaged investment accounts hands-off. Always keep them growing for your future.

- *an unsolicited supply of blank checks in your mailbox,* courtesy of your credit card company, with your name and address already imprinted. The pitch is that you can avoid the hassle of using a credit card by simply making these checks payable to your favorite store or even to yourself for a quick infusion of cash. The amount will be added to the balance due on your credit card. (What is not clear, unless you have a magnifying glass to read it, is that interest accrues from the moment your check is posted; there is no grace period even if your account is paid in full.) It's a bad deal all around: Your benevolent credit card company has placed temptation in your hands, with an interest arrangement that tilts the deal even more in its favor. It has also put you at considerable security risk, for anyone could tear open the envelope and use those checks. Don't fall for convenient checks in the mail. Tear them up as soon as you receive them. Then call the credit card company and instruct it to remove your name from its pitch list.

- *a credit card backed by the equity in your home.* In other words, a home-equity line of credit with a credit card to make impulse spending more convenient. Again, don't do it. A home-equity line should be used carefully, cautiously—and only for appreciating assets such as home improvement. You should never use credit, especially credit backed by your home, for consumable or depreciating items. It's just plain lousy stewardship. And if you get in too deep and are unable to pay, you could lose your house.

- *TV shopping channels and infomercials.* They've hired professional persuaders whose sole purpose is to convince you that you must "call now!" Did you notice that they don't take checks? Need I say more?

- *rationalization.* As you break free of consumer debt, you can always count on temptation to try to pull you back. You may even catch yourself devising some of the most logical-sounding rationalizations for continuing to feed the monster: "It's on sale!" "I owe it to myself." "We've been good—we'll splurge a little." "We'll pay it off at the end of the month. Or the next."

Stand Strong against Temptation

Even when you've worked so diligently to eliminate consumer debt, the forces of this world will do everything they can to pull you back into the trap. Stand strong. Earmark the money you had been sending to creditors for redirection to your personal savings and investments. Here are some ways to help you keep your commitment:

- *Stick to the one-card rule.* That's all you'll need from here on. Shred all invitations for additional cards, and write the companies asking them to remove you from their mailing lists.

- *Determine the maximum you will charge to your one card in a given month.* With your spouse, agree on a modest monthly dollar limit that you will not go beyond, no matter what "opportunities" may come your way. It should be a sum you feel you can comfortably pay *in full* upon arrival of the monthly statement without sacrificing any other areas of your budget. Need a number? Start at $30 per month, max. If you find yourself going beyond that, or not paying the statement in full at the end of each month, it's scissors time again.

- *Ask yourself some tough questions.* The fact that you've determined a maximum monthly limit for credit card spending does not *obligate* you to spend that much every month. So when the urge for unplanned credit card spending rears its seductive head (and it will), ask yourself some tough questions to see if the alluring expenditure is really necessary: *Why do I want this? Is it a whim I'll regret in a week? Will I want this item as badly in thirty days when the bill comes?*

- *Pay each credit card purchase in full upon the arrival of the statement.* Without exception, do not allow payment of any charges to be delayed to a future month. A practical way to accomplish this objective is to actually deduct a credit card purchase from your checking-account ledger on the same day you incur the obligation. Make a clear note to yourself regarding the purchase, *circle it,* then deduct the amount of the purchase from your checking-account total. When the credit card statement arrives, the total of your circled items should be the same as the total of the month's credit card charges. Since the funds have already been deducted from your checking-account ledger, you'll be able to write a check to the credit card company paying your new charges in full.

- *Avoid future debt burdens and finance charges by saving in advance for major purchases.* Disciplined debt management enables you to be much more aggressive in your savings program. And by saving in advance for future needs, you can help prevent future debt obligations and costly finance charges. So if you haven't already done so, now's the time to begin setting money aside in your money-market fund for all those wonderful things the nice bank wanted you to charge to your very own platinum credit card. From now on, you're going to pay cash, from checking or savings, for all depreciating or consumable items.

- *If you find you're still running up your one card, it's scissors time again.* If the safe-deposit box or frozen milk carton doesn't cure you of credit card co-dependency, your course is clear: Take the offending credit card and give it the scissors treatment. You don't need that source of credit; it's doing you more harm than good. Slash it up; pay it off; shut it down. From now on, let your debit card be your means of payment when you can't write a check or pay cash. Properly used, it will help impose the discipline you need to stay current.

It's Worth the Effort!

When you keep consumer debt under control, you'll feel a greater sense of security, control, and peace of mind. You won't feel so strapped between paychecks; your monthly cash flow will be enhanced. You will have more discretionary dollars the following month, enabling you to purchase with cash instead of expensive credit. You will build a savings reserve to cover true emergencies and to pay up-front for vacations and other major purchases. You'll be able to invest more diligently for the long term so you'll be financially independent when retirement comes—free from dependence on the government and your children. Most important, as you better provide for your family and your future, you'll also be able to give more to a worthy cause in your community, to your church, or to someone in need.

And we're not just thinking "years down the road." Blast away at debt, stay true to your resolve, and you'll begin reaping the rewards right away. You will truly understand what we mean when we say, *Stop borrowing trouble—for good.*

Ignoring the Money-Body Connection

If you live like there's no tomorrow,
you may be right.

It can't happen to you—until it does.

Heart disease, our nation's number one killer, claims nearly half a million men and women each year. Those it doesn't kill, it debilitates—millions of us, possibly you or someone you know. If you live with heart disease, you know too well the constant, hovering fear that every day, every moment, every breath could be your last. And you're all too aware of the way heart disease crimps the lifestyles of your loved ones and of its devastating effect on personal finances.

Cancer, in one form or another, is the second-leading cause of death in the United States. The American Institute for Cancer Research estimates that one in two men and one in three women will develop some form of cancer—alarming odds, considering that ours is supposed to be among the most technologically and medically advanced nations of the world. If you've encountered cancer on a personal level, whether in your own family or in the life of another loved one, you know its horrible effects. There's no way to paste a pretty picture over how this disease erodes the body, mind, and spirit of the patient and his or her loved ones—and no way to gloss over the heavy toll it can take on their personal finances as well.

But this type of thing happens only to other people, right? Sure, we read about it, see reports on TV news magazines, and perhaps even know and care deeply for someone who has died from or is fighting a major illness. But it's not really until heart disease, cancer, or another life-wrenching disease invades our personal space—our own lives or those of our nuclear or extended families—that we realize that, yes, it indeed *can* happen to us. And it does.

You may be wondering why I'm devoting a segment of a book about personal finance to a subject such as debilitating disease. I wish I could avoid it—I really do. I don't enjoy thinking about these things any more than you do. However, the physical, emotional, and financial devastation of ill health is too prevalent to ignore. As I write this, a good friend of mine is entering the hospital for quadruple coronary bypass surgery. Another is being ravaged by severe, most likely terminal, cancer. A few years ago my father left our presence too soon, one of the growing number of victims of malignant melanoma. Several years before that, Dad nursed my mom through a triple coronary bypass. (She's led a full life since, though she is somewhat limited by the lingering after-effects of the surgery.) Another dear relative, though spry and mobile, is on oxygen twenty-four hours each day to help ease the results of congestive heart failure. Nearly every fellow baby boomer I've talked with recently is concerned about a parent who struggles with heart disease, cancer in some form, or other serious health problems.

It *can* happen to us. And when it does, it's devastating. Not just physically and emotionally, but financially.

Poor Health Costs Good Money

And that's why we must speak plainly about health issues here—because poor health costs good money. It can eat away at our financial reserves or even wipe them out, forcing the postponement of needs, goals, and dreams. For retirees, out-of-pocket health-care costs can seriously reduce the nest eggs from which they draw their living expenses. Even those of us fortunate enough to carry "good" medical insurance find that health issues consume increasing percentages of cash flow due to skyrocketing deductibles, co-pays, and no-pays. As the costs of medical treatment and prescription drugs soar, insurers find more and more excuses to decline or reduce payment.

For all these reasons, the cost of health care has become one of the primary concerns of the aging population. So as I help you put strategies in place to build financial independence for the future, I would be remiss if I didn't encourage you to contemplate the financial impact of ill health and to take every step you can to be as healthy as possible. Granted, serious illness isn't always the result of cause and effect. While many illnesses are the clear result of unhealthy lifestyle choices such as smoking, drinking, drug abuse, and poor dietary and exercise habits, other maladies encroach for no apparent rhyme or reason. Regardless of how careful we are, there's no guarantee we'll go disease-free; as Sean Connery said while charging headlong into a gun battle in *The Untouchables*, "We all gotta die of somethin'." However, we *can* take steps to proactively steer clear of the stupid, unhealthy lifestyle choices that practically guarantee a reduction in quality of life as well as a serious erosion of our life savings.

Your Body and Your Money

Just in case you're still doubtful of the relationship between wellness and your personal finances, consider these thoughts regarding the physical-fiscal connection:

- *When you're out of shape, your mind and body lack the alertness and endurance you need to be at your best all day, day in and day out.* This affects not only your performance but also your attitude. Most of us may be able to fake it through a tough day or two but not for an extended length of time. Lethargy and a poor attitude quickly drain the quality and efficiency of your work and are obvious to your leaders and peers. On the other hand, good health keeps the mind and body fresh, alert, and strong. Physically, mentally, emotionally, and spiritually, you feel more energetic and upbeat. You process questions more positively and effectively. You require fewer sick days. You approach problems and challenges with a positive, can-do spirit. A sound mind and strong body help you do your job well. When you do your job well, you not only hold on to your job, but you also enhance your chances of winning promotions and raises—all of which supply the income you need to provide for your family and save and invest for your future.

- *Stupid healthstyle choices wear down your body's immune system.* Eating the wrong foods, getting too little sleep, letting stress dam up inside you, failing to exercise consistently—all combine to batter down your inner reserves. Sooner or later your immune system's going to shriek, "Unfair! On strike!" You may try to ignore the illness and work on, perhaps even self-medicating at $12.99 a pop, courtesy of your grocery's drug aisle, but forging ahead only wears you down further. Eventually you miss a day or more of work. You drag yourself to the doctor, who charges $85 just for a parking space and after a thorough two-minute examination scrawls a prescription costing you another $30 if your insurance covers it and up to $120 if it does not. You'll likely recover, but it's already cost you time and goodwill at work and cash out of your pocket. Down the road, the cumulative effect of your bad habits could dent or even drain your life savings if you're flattened by a major illness such as heart disease, stroke, or cancer. In contrast, if you invest a bit of time, effort, and discipline now to begin trading in those poor choices for good ones, you'll enjoy immediate benefits of alertness, endurance, and vitality. You'll also have the peace of mind that comes from knowing that your new lifestyle choices will likely help avoid huge, asset-draining medical expenses down the road.

- *Much as we hate to admit it, we're all growing older.* Back in your teens and twenties, middle age and senior citizenship seemed so far away, didn't they? But now, suddenly, they are *here or just around the corner.* Each year seems to rush by faster than the last. As you draw closer to retirement age, you naturally begin to wonder if your health will allow you to truly enjoy the golden years. You don't want to be bedridden or housebound, your dreams curtailed or your days cut short by untimely, debilitating illness. Good health will help supply the energy and vitality you'll need to enjoy an active, fully engaged life. Smart, healthy choices now will help empower you physically and conserve your financial ability to truly make the most of the rest of your life.

Of Cheese, Chocolate, and Caffeine

While I've managed to steer clear of obviously harmful choices such as smoking, alcohol, and drug abuse, I don't pretend to be an expert or even a role model when it comes to health and nutrition. I've made my share of stupid healthstyle choices. Cheese and chocolate, both high in artery-clogging saturated fat, are two of my favorite vices. I've made a genuine, mostly effective effort to keep consumption at modest levels. (A few years back I whooped with delight when a scientific study announced that chocolate was good for the heart—until I read the fine print and learned that the study had been sponsored by the chocolate industry.)

Too much caffeine can elevate blood pressure and chew away at the stomach lining, yet I don't consider myself awake in the morning until I've consumed a cup of this wonderful life-giving fluid. And once or twice a week I'll even take out a second mortgage on the house to finance a *venti* Starbucks nonfat caramel macchiato. But I've recognized the error of my earlier days and have reduced coffee consumption from four or five cups per day (I may as well have set up an IV drip) to one or two.

In my teens and early adulthood, I chose, more by ignorance than intent, to internalize stress instead of relaxing and talking or working it out. The result was a stomach ulcer at the tender age of thirty-one. The ulcer cleared up in a few weeks and hasn't revisited, but it was a sobering wake-up call telling me that I needed to improve at keeping life's challenges in perspective (it's *all* small stuff). I needed to commit to laugh more and worry less, to stay in better physical shape, and to be more discerning in what I slammed down my gullet.

Kathy and I are now in our early fifties and, short of the normal dings of growing older, we enjoy good health—for which we're deeply grateful. We realize this could change in an instant, and we do not take wellness for granted. It's an ongoing commitment, a never-ending series of moment-by-moment healthstyle choices.

When we overrule unhealthy decisions with healthy ones, we feel so much more vital, energetic, and upbeat—so much better equipped to enjoy the great adventure called life. I'm confident you will too. With that goal in mind, as well as the financial objective of having to spend fewer dollars to treat illness now and in the future, please consider the following ten life-enhancing choices that will help you take charge of your health and help ensure a life of vitality for you and your loved ones.

Ten Smart Choices for a Long, Healthy Life

1. Make water your favorite beverage.

Four out of five nutritionists agree that water is the most essential nutrient in the body. (The fifth nutritionist was from the planet Gelkor, a waterless planet.) Water carries nutrients to the cells and dilutes and flushes toxins from the body. It lubricates joints and organs, forms blood and other bodily fluids, and promotes regularity. It is essential to the formation and repair of tissue and to the chemical reactions our bodies require.

Approximately 60 percent of the human body is fluid, and studies have found that losing just 5 percent of our body fluid can cause painful headaches, fatigue, forgetfulness, elevated pulse rate, and confusion (which may explain the nutritionist from Gelkor). We lose 2.5 to 3 percent of our bodies' water supply through urination and perspiration—more during strenuous exercise—so it is essential that we be proactive in replenishing our internal water supply.

Nutritionists recommend that we drink a minimum of eight tall glasses of water each day. But if you're not accustomed to sipping water all day long, this recommended minimum may seem unmanageable. How do you do it? First, rehydrate your system after the night's fast by slamming down a tall, cold glass of water immediately upon rising in the morning, before you jump in the shower or begin your morning mirror routine. Have another as you're fixing breakfast. Then keep fresh, cold water at your work station during the day; drink one or two glassfuls during the morning. Enjoy another with lunch and another during the afternoon. Have a tall glass of water with dinner, then one in the evening. That's eight. If you exercise (and I hope you do), sip more water before, during, and after each workout.

2. Give yourself a break.

Keep the steam-release valve open on your pressure cooker by taking frequent minibreaks during the day. If possible, step away from your work station (go outside if the weather permits); shift your mind into neutral; do some slow, deep breathing; and stretch to loosen your neck, shoulder, and back muscles. You'll feel refreshed after just a couple of minutes. When possible, take a vigorous walk during your lunch break.

If you're among the millions who tend to take work home with you—in your mind if not in your briefcase—be sure you extend this practice into late afternoon or evening with a consistent exercise program. In other words . . .

3. Work it out.

I'm not talking about additional labor at the office—you already devote enough of your week to that. By "working it out" I'm referring to a brisk thirty-minute walk, jog, bike ride, or aerobic workout at least three days each week for your cardiovascular system. On alternating days, balance aerobics with a moderate resistance workout with dumbbells, barbells, or weight machines to enhance strength and muscle tone. The combination will help you lose weight; increase strength, energy, and vitality; and ease tension over the crises and stresses of your day. There's also increasing evidence that regular, vigorous exercise releases endorphins and other natural chemicals into the bloodstream to combat pain and strengthen the immune system against disease.

4. Go to bed.

Are you getting enough sleep? Just a few years ago, "enlightened" scientists were proclaiming that the time-tested advice was all wrong, that we don't really need eight hours of sleep each night. Then, apparently cranky from too-little sleep, they reversed themselves and declared that Mom was right all along: Most of us indeed need at least eight hours' sleep, and we're not getting it. We are, in fact, resoundingly sleep-deprived, which may help explain anxiety, depression, road rage, exhaustion on the job, and some of the stupid things we do with our money. Sound sleep—at least eight hours' worth—is foundational to physical, mental, and emotional vitality.

What choices do you need to make to get the sleep you need? What two adjustments can you make in your life to get to bed thirty to sixty minutes earlier and/or rise a half-hour later?

5. Eat for life.

Recent reports indicate that more than 60 percent of American adults are overweight, which is a diplomatic way of saying, "We're fat." We eat when we need to but also when we don't. We eat to be social and when we feel antisocial. We eat to celebrate anything, and we eat when we're anxious, depressed, or bored.

In other words, when in doubt, we eat. And when we do, we tend to eat heavily processed foods loaded with carcinogenic chemicals, artery-clogging saturated fats, and colon-rotting sugars . . . because they're convenient and they taste good going down. As a result, we're overweight, unfit, and susceptible to disease—which not only diminishes our joy of life but also translates into higher health-care costs now and in years to come.

You can counter the destructive effects of poor food choices by determining that whenever you do eat, you'll "eat for life" by selecting smart, healthy, delicious alternatives: foods that cleanse instead of clog, that defend instead of destroy. Studies show the following foods to be especially effective in supplying your body and brain with the nutrients they need for strength and efficiency—while helping prevent problems such as heart disease, cancer, diabetes, and stroke:

- brightly colored fresh fruits and vegetables—nutritionists recommend several servings of each every day
- whole grains such as brown rice, multi-grain breads, and oats
- beans and legumes
- nuts (especially raw almonds and walnuts) and seeds
- soybeans and soy products
- salmon, tuna, herring, mackerel, and sardines
- green and black tea

In recent years scientists have also confirmed that contemporary society is under constant assault by harmful free-radical chemicals ("oxidants") that can debilitate our internal organs and other cell tissue long before their time. Antioxidants, which include beta carotene, selenium, and vitamins C and E, are crucial to the immune system and cellular integrity and also promote healing. Fortunately, our Creator has provided many delicious, natural antioxidants, including prunes, raisins, blueberries, blackberries, red grapes, cranberries, strawberries, and raspberries. Any of these fruits can be easily added to your morning oatmeal or other whole-grain cereal. You can also drink antioxidants in the form of 100 percent cranberry juice or unsweetened grape juice (why add sugar when it's naturally sweet?). Green tea is also high in antioxidants and can provide a pleasant, soothing effect.

Two other nuggets of good advice when it comes to eating for life:

- Read the ingredients list of any food or beverage you're about to buy. The longer the list of ingredients, the more likely it is that the item will do you more harm than good.

- If the ingredients label lists "high fructose corn syrup" or "partially hydrogenated" anything, return the item to the shelf and choose a healthy alternative. This will eliminate many of the typical fruit drinks and snack foods purchased by well-meaning moms every week, but it will also open your horizons to a vast world of delicious, healthy foods and beverages.

6. Conquer an unhealthy habit.

If you smoke, you don't need to be told about the horrible things you're doing to your body and to your loved ones who must inhale the cancer with you. Unless you stop *right now*, you're destined for years of wheezing and gasping and possible lung cancer unless a stroke or heart attack takes you sooner. Either way, your family and your finances will suffer. Of all the healthstyle mistakes we can make, smoking has to be at the top of the list because the word has been out for years on how harmful this stupid habit is.

On the other hand, the benefits of quitting are remarkable—and almost immediate. When you cease a pack-a-day habit, you're suddenly saving about $100 per month. Put those monthly savings to work in an IRA averaging just 8 percent per year, and over twenty years it'll compound to almost $59,000. Grow healthier and grow richer! More importantly, you'll begin to feel better within days of quitting—you'll breathe a little easier, feel more lively and alert, and experience greater endurance. Combine smoking cessation with regular exercise, and you'll be delighted at your newfound vitality. (You'll also smell better, for which family, friends, and coworkers will be grateful.)

You May Be Making Stupid Mistake #6 If . . .

○ you allow the stresses of life to build up inside you

○ you engage in concentrated exercise fewer than three days per week

○ you haven't had a physical exam in two years or more

○ you smoke or hang around those who do

○ you don't take a multivitamin and mineral supplement

○ your broad mind and narrow waist are trading places

If you're not a smoker, perhaps there's another harmful habit you struggle with—much as I'm tempted by cheese, chocolate, and coffee. If so, be honest with yourself: Which habit do you feel the least control over? Choose one harmful healthstyle choice that you'd like to change for the better—take on just one for now—and dedicate yourself to making the change permanent.

To encourage you, I'll share another personal example. Since Kathy and I both love chocolate, we've always kept it around the house. A few years ago we realized that we had gone far beyond moderate consumption. We'd grab some after meals and between meals, then another helping while watching a TV program in the evening. Between the two of us (mostly me), we could go through a large bag of M&M's in four or five days (two to three of the almond variety). It felt so good going down, but we'd feel so sluggish afterward. Finally we decided that we had to ease off this stupid habit and that the best way to do so was to keep chocolate out of the house. We made a fun wager: The first person to bring home chocolate must pay the other a $10 fine. (We're both stubborn enough that we're not about to owe the other such a penalty.) We determined that we'd make chocolate a special, occasional treat when we dine out instead of the everyday "entitlement" it had become.

I thought we'd go through severe withdrawal, much like alcoholics on the wagon, but there were no tremors, no hallucinations, no homicides. We started feeling better immediately. We didn't miss our daily "fix." Before we knew it, we'd been practicing our new discipline for an entire year. Not only were we cleansing the sugary junk from our systems, but we were also saving approximately $5 each week and redirecting it toward better things.

Before you read any further, I heartily encourage you to think of one stupid healthstyle habit in your life that is not only harmful to your health but is also harmful to your budget. Write it down and take it on. Make the change permanent. Revel in your newfound vitality and redirect the money you were spending to something positive, such as debt elimination or increased savings for your future.

7. Laugh.

Several years back, author Norman Cousins set the medical establishment on its ear with his groundbreaking book, *Anatomy of an Illness*. It told how, after doctors had given him little hope of overcoming a debilitating disease, Cousins found healing in laughter. Despite physical agony and exhaustion from the ravages of the illness, he watched movie after movie of the Marx Brothers, Laurel and Hardy, and other classic comedies—and he laughed. He laughed so much that his body hurt less . . . and less . . . and he regained his functionality for several more years.

We now know that the laughter was releasing powerful endorphins to strengthen both mind and body. If endorphins are that strong in combating actual illness and agony, imagine what they can do to help strengthen and rejuvenate us in the midst of everyday stresses. All we need to do is laugh and let them do their job.

Remember, life is all small stuff. Look for the humor in every situation and find something to laugh about. Laughter will help clear and relax your mind as you weigh solutions to your problems; it'll ease bodily tension and help you keep things in perspective. Laughter is one of God's provisions to help you stay healthy and strong.

8. Supplement your nutrition.

Many nutritional specialists believe that in our stressful, polluted world, good foods alone do not supply the full amounts of vitamins, minerals, and other nutrients we need. Thus it makes sense to supplement our diets each day with a high-potency multivitamin and mineral formula. As we grow older, we'll want to pay special attention to our intake of calcium for bone density and to vitamins C and E, beta carotene, and selenium for their antioxidant benefits.

Much has also been documented regarding the effectiveness of certain herbal supplements such as Ginkgo biloba for enhanced mental alertness; St. John's wort for emotional stability; and phytoestrogen, a kinder, gentler hormone-replacement therapy for women in midlife. It should be noted that some herbal supplements do not combine well with certain prescription drugs, so if you take prescription medication, be sure to check with your doctor before trying an herbal supplement.

9. Get away from it all—soon and often.

Considering the intensity of the typical American workload, one to three weeks of vacation out of fifty-two is chump change—hardly enough to truly relax, rejuvenate, and refresh for long-haul effectiveness. Add to that the guilt most of us feel over taking that well-deserved vacation, the length of time it takes to stop thinking about work, and our orders (or inner compulsions) to stay in touch with the workplace while away, and it's little wonder that we return to work almost as tired as when we left.

A psychologist friend of mine contends that America is centuries behind Europe and other parts of the world when it comes to vacations and holidays. We take one to three weeks; they take six to eight. In search of excellence, we work harder and longer; they break away to relax and refresh. Which is truly most effective? Which course is wiser and healthier? Could it be that vacation-stingy employers and workaholic employees actually do each other more harm than good?

Alas, you and I may not be able to change the vacation policies at our places of employment, but we can take full advantage of what vacation time we do have. Do not entertain an inkling of guilt about taking every moment you're entitled to. You've more than earned it. Get away from it all—truly *away*. Inform your colleagues that you will not be available by phone or e-mail, then leave your cell phone, pager, and laptop computer at home. Enjoy your family and the world outside your window; inhale the blessing of rejuvenation. Breaking away to rest and rejuvenate is one of life's best investments.

10. Be proactive with your health.

We've all heard of the importance of self-examination of breasts, testicles, or skin moles for abnormalities. However, I suspect the reason so many of us resist taking these simple proactive measures is that we're afraid of what we could find. In view of the possibilities, we'd rather put off self-examination for another day—or forget it altogether and hope for the best.

The good news is that, quite often, abnormalities and even some cancers are highly treatable *when detected and treated early*. The key is early detection, and in most cases this is up to us because of the infrequency of our visits to medical specialists.

When my dad died of malignant melanoma, I suddenly became much more observant of skin moles and more conscientious about the use of sunscreen. I also began scheduling semiannual visits with my M.D. for thorough examinations of any moles that appear suspicious. He checks every inch of my body—from the scalp to the bottom of my feet—aided by a bright light and magnifying glass. He tells me that skin cancer is on an alarming upswing throughout the country and that one cannot be too careful. Melanoma, when detected early, is highly treatable. Once it metastasizes, however, one's chances of survival are slim.

For women, regular self-examination of breasts is of course a vital proactive measure. For men, regular self-examination of the testicles for abnormal lumps can be performed easily while showering. If anything feels abnormal or different from your last self-exam, see your physician immediately. If it's serious, your chances of successful treatment will be far greater because you detected it early. If it's nothing, you'll enjoy the wonderful peace of mind that comes from a clean bill of health.

Of course, no one should rely exclusively on self-examination. None of us enjoys the sundry pokes and prods that go with visits to the doctor, but those regular physical exams, including mammograms and pap smears for women and prostate exams for men, are essential to the stewardship of our health as we grow older. If your physician spots a potential problem, he or she can check it out further and, if necessary, administer treatment. If you're pronounced healthy, you'll gain an extra measure of confidence and peace of mind.

Most doctors recommend a preventive exam at least every two years through our forties, then once each year thereafter. You'll need to be proactive because, unlike insurance agents and grinning car salesmen, M.D.'s generally don't advertise or send reminders. It's initiative worth taking. Place your own reminders in your long-range planning calendar and call faithfully to schedule appointments. Make your doctor a team-mate in your commitment to wellness.

Pay Now or Pay Later

I trust that this chapter has helped you better understand the close interaction between your physical habits and your financial well-being. Bottom line: Poor healthstyle choices can lead to lousy finances, both now and down the road. But by taking charge of your health today, you can help steer clear of those cost-prohibitive, debilitating problems later in life.

Failure to Use Your Four Powerful Friends

A friend is a present you give yourself.

—Robert Louis Stevenson

He had earned a steady, above-average income his entire career. Now, in his early fifties, Jeremy was finally taking time to assess what he had to show for all his hard work—and what he needed to do in order to ensure that he'd have the financial freedom to retire in the next fifteen or twenty years.

Over the years, Jeremy had tucked away extra money in a money market fund whenever his cash flow allowed. He had built up a contingency reserve of $4,200, which he tried to leave alone. He considered this his "fallback" reserve in case of a job loss or other expensive emergency.

He carried balances totaling $2,600 on three of his four credit cards and tried to pay at least $250 each month on those balances. But Jeremy admitted that he often found himself putting additional purchases on his credit cards, which made paying down the balances more difficult. He also owed approximately $5,500 on a car loan, which brought his total consumer debt to $8,100.

Jeremy's company offered a 401(k), to which he contributed 5 percent of his $50,000 gross income, or $2,500 per year. A few years ago he had borrowed from the plan to take a special vacation, and he now was almost finished making the required payback of the loan.

"Let's See What's Holding You Back"

The first thing I did was to commend Jeremy on the things he was doing right. He had built a rainy-day reserve that he kept set aside, yet available, in a money-market fund. He was making a concerted effort to pay down his consumer debt. And, mindful of retiring someday, he was contributing to his company 401(k).

"Now," I told him, "let's see what's holding you back." Among other things, we underscored the following:

First, while his contingency reserve was a good beginning, it needed shoring up. At his present level of monthly expenses, Jeremy's rainy-day fund would provide only about six weeks' living expenses if he were to lose his job. He needed to build and maintain this reserve at a level that could see him through at least three months of potential unemployment.

Second, while Jeremy was not overly abusing his lines of consumer credit, his credit card balances and car loan totaled 16 percent of his gross income—more than three times our recommended maximum consumer debt of 5 percent. He was flushing away hundreds of dollars each month in expensive debt service, money that he could and should have been pouring into his savings programs.

Third, while participation in his company's 401(k) was commendable, Jeremy was failing to utilize the plan's full potential. He'd made the cardinal error of borrowing from his retirement savings, which had dramatically reduced his balance as well as his potential for compounding. And while his plan allowed for a maximum annual contribution of up to 15 percent of gross salary, Jeremy was contributing only 5 percent. By not maxing out his 401(k) contributions, he was saving $5,000 less per year than the plan allowed.

The math quickly revealed why this third shortcoming was a big one. At only 5 percent of his gross income of $50,000, Jeremy was sending just $208.33 to his 401(k) each month. Invested in a portfolio of mutual funds averaging 8 percent earnings over the next fifteen years, and assuming no increases in his monthly contributions, his new contributions would compound to a total of $72,090. But if Jeremy were to begin to contribute the full 15 percent allowed by his plan, $416.67 per month, his new contributions would grow to a total of $144,184 (again, assuming no increases in pay or monthly contributions). The difference: an additional $72,094 in his retirement fund fifteen years from now. And as contribution limits increase over time, he can enhance these results even more.

Your Four Powerful Friends

"You have four powerful financial friends," I assured Jeremy. "They're there for you, but you're not using them. They can make you wealthy over time, but you've got to put them to work."

Over the next several months, as Jeremy began to make adjustments to his personal finances, he came to know and love his four powerful friends. For the next fifteen years, until the day he hoped to retire, these friends would help make the dramatic difference between whether he would *strive* or *thrive* in his retirement years.

As I have emphasized throughout this book, you and I are mostly on our own when it comes to building economic security for our families and for our future. It is up to us to take positive steps *now* to overcome any Stupid Mistakes of the past and to steer clear of them in the future. It is up to us to get out and stay out of the consumer-debt trap, to build an accessible contingency reserve for life's inevitable rainy days, and to save and invest a healthy portion of every dollar for future needs and dreams.

No one else will take these steps for us. We're on our own. This is a key financial reality we all must face, and the sooner the better.

We can reject that reality, pine passively for the illusive Someday, and arrive at our retirement years dependent upon government, children, or charity. Or we can embrace the reality, determine the best ways to work with and make the most of it, and dramatically enhance our chances of becoming financially free to make our retirement years the most active, productive, and fulfilling time of our lives.

I think I know which choice you've made. And, assuming you've chosen the path to financial freedom, I have more encouraging news for you—news that will give you even greater hope of reaching your destination in sound fiscal shape: While you are on your own, you are not alone.

Huh?

You read that correctly. It's not a contradiction.

Yes, it's up to you to assume the initiative, take the right steps, and maintain the discipline to see your plan through. No one will force you to do these important things, and no one will do them for you. Indeed, you are on your own. But on the other hand, like Jeremy, you have powerful friends who can help make your financial goal a reality.

I'm not talking about your parents, who may or may not have any money to leave to you.

Not Bill Gates, who has money but probably didn't remember you in his will.

And not your rich, eccentric Uncle Fester, who intends to leave his money to his cats.

Before you meet your powerful friends, let me illustrate their value by comparing your financial life to a football game. You're a running back on a football team (so, humor me here). It's your responsibility to take the ball and run through the opposition toward the goal line. The opposing players are drooling to stop you, even lay some serious pain on you. But (thank God) you are not the only player on your team. You have some powerful teammates, hard-hitting blockers who can help spring you loose for significant gains and game-winning touchdowns. You're carrying the ball on your own, but as you run toward the goal line, you are not alone.

Now relate that metaphor to the game of personal finance.

You're journeying toward a goal. Opposing forces want to stop you and even lay some financial pain on you. But you have powerful "teammates" who can help you make the most of your efforts to build financial independence. Working together, they can take a fistful of your dollars and help them grow and multiply. They can help turn what may seem a small puddle of savings into a full reservoir to fund a thriving retirement.

When it comes to building financial freedom, these teammates are going to be your four best friends.

The Power of Priority

Priority is a watchword that conveys moving something from the bottom of a to-do list to the top. It changes an action step from an afterthought ("Someday") to one of utmost importance ("Today!"). If you're a husband, cleaning the garage may be at the bottom of your list. But your dear wife has grown tired of having to scale boxes and yard tools to get to her car, and this morning she announced that cleaning the garage had better be your top priority this weekend. If you want to stay fed and out of the doghouse, you'd better make a paradigm shift, and fast. Suddenly you move cleaning the garage from the bottom to the top of your to-do list. You shift this task from afterthought to priority. The garage gets cleaned (finally!), and you're assured of another meal indoors.

That's the power of priority. It gets things done that we may have previously considered undesirable, unimportant, or impossible. We touched upon this powerful principle earlier when we talked about the importance of making savings and investing a top-priority habit instead of a financial afterthought. Instead of paying all of your other bills and seeing if there's anything left for savings at the end of the pay period, *the power of priority* puts a permanent paradigm shift into play: You designate a percentage of your income for savings and investment and set up an automatic transfer program to make sure you "pay yourself first." In doing so, you move savings and investment from the bottom of the list to the top. The only financial practice that should top regular savings and investment is that of charitable giving.

When I speak to groups about personal finance, I occasionally share a tongue-in-cheek statement that actually underscores this key financial principle. "I'll say this slowly because I want you to write down every word," I tell them. Everyone puts pen to paper, poised to record the coming nugget of wisdom. "Here it is: *The odds of making a successful investment are dramatically increased . . . if you have some money to invest in the first place.*"

By the time I complete that last phrase, most of the group pause momentarily and glance up from their notes, as if wondering whether they should finish writing. Then, invariably, they smile as they realize that, indeed, *we can't put money to work for the future if we don't first set aside the money to put to work.* We cannot afford to save only whenever we have some extra cash because—be honest—how often does that happen?

We have to build the seed capital. Regularly and systematically, early and often.

That's where paying ourselves first comes in.

The power of priority.

Seed money won't just come along Someday. Successful investors *create* seed money by having it skimmed from their income automatically, before they can spend it on anything else. This moves savings from the bottom of the to-do list to the top. Employer-sponsored programs such as 401(k)s are ideal, tax-advantaged ways to make this happen. In addition, you can arrange for automatic transfers from your paycheck or your checking account to your personal IRA or other savings and investment program.

How much should you be saving?

As much as you can, which is more than you think you can.

To review Stupid Mistake #2, your initial savings priority should be to build and maintain a contingency reserve of three to six months' living expenses. A good place for this reserve is a money-market fund. Once you have a good start in building that reserve, you'll also want to begin saving toward medium-term expenses such as a down payment on your first house or your children's college education.

Your *biggest* future expense, however, is likely to be your retirement. Considering increased life spans as well as advances in health and medicine, it's possible that you could live in retirement mode (translation: mostly self-supporting) for twenty-five, thirty, or even forty years. That's a long time to make your money last. To build a nest egg large enough to live out your days in financial independence, it is vital that you put the power of priority to work for you. Begin *now*, no matter how young or old you are, to set aside a portion of every paycheck for your future. I recommend the following as a good, minimum rule of thumb:

- Up to age thirty-five, steer at least 5 *percent* of your gross income to retirement savings.

- Between ages thirty-five and forty-five, save at least 10 *percent* for retirement.

- From ages forty-five to fifty-five, save at least 15 *percent* of your gross income for retirement.

- After age fifty-five, save at least 20 *percent* for retirement.

Such a time line should allow you to save for short- and medium-term needs in your early years, while also getting a good start on saving for the long term. Gradually, as you complete your contingency reserve, make the down payment on your first house, and move your children out of the nest, you can save more aggressively for retirement. But every working person should be saving *something* for retirement, no matter how young he or she may be. The sooner you begin, the better off you're likely to be as retirement approaches.

If you do not harness the power of priority in your savings and investment practices, chances are you'll experience difficulty building sufficient seed capital to invest for your future. But if you begin today to make savings one of your top financial priorities, you'll have the money to put to work. That's where your next powerful friend comes into play.

The Power of Tax-Advantaged Saving

"I'm from the IRS, and I'm here to help you."

Yeah, right. If you ever hear that, it will be in your dreams.

Yet, difficult as it may be to believe, our government has actually stepped forward to help us when it comes to saving for retirement. (It's their way of admitting that there's no way Social Security will meet all of our retirement-income needs and that we'd better save on our own—and fast.) Be still, my heart; Uncle Sam actually wants to encourage us to save for the long term by giving us some generous tax breaks for doing so.

Tax-advantaged saving means that (1) your contribution to your savings plan is tax-deductible in the year you make it or (2) earnings on your investments are tax-deferred until you withdraw funds or (3) both. One or both of these benefits give us the significant *advantage* of keeping more of our money compounding for us in lieu of sending it to Washington to buy $10,000 toilet seats.

With tax-advantaged savings vehicles such as 401(k)s, 403(b)s, SEP-IRAs, and some traditional IRAs, the money we put into these programs can be deducted from our gross income at tax time. (The much-bally-hooed Roth IRA does not allow you to deduct your contribution, but it offers other benefits that make it a strong retirement savings vehicle in its own right. We'll review those benefits in a later chapter.)

Through *tax deductibility*, our government actually encourages us to save for retirement by, in effect, subsidizing our contributions to these long-term savings vehicles. If your income level puts you in the 15 percent marginal tax bracket and you authorize your employer to direct a total of $3,000 of your gross salary to your company 401(k), you will pay $450 less in federal income tax than if you do not make the tax-deductible contribution. In effect, you'll contribute just $2,550; Uncle Sam tosses in $450 for you because of your tax savings. If you're in the 28 percent marginal bracket and you decide to set aside $6,000, you will effectively contribute $4,320 while the government contributes $1,680 in tax savings. The more you contribute up to the legal limit, the more you can deduct from your income tax. It's like being paid to save—yet, amazingly, hundreds of thousands of men and women who have such plans available do not take advantage of them or contribute the full amount they are entitled to save.

An even more powerful tax advantage is that of *tax deferral*. Annuities, 401(k)s, 403(b)s, SEP-IRAs, Roth IRAs, and traditional IRAs all allow us to postpone paying taxes on their investment earnings until we begin drawing income from them.

Consider tax deferral a way to "turbocharge" the already-powerful effect of compounding on your savings and investments. Because compounding earns interest on principal *and interest on interest*, sheltering your earnings from annual taxation means you can keep more money growing for you over time.

First you exercise the power of priority to set a healthy percentage of your income aside for the future. Then you take Uncle Sam up on the power of tax-advantaged saving in order to legally avoid taxes and keep more of your money working for you. Now it's time for your third powerful financial friend . . .

The Power of Equity Investing

Equity investing enables you to invest a portion of your saved money for growth over time, enhancing its opportunity to surpass the growth you would have achieved had you left it all in a low-earning savings account or money-market fund.

To help you become comfortable with this powerful friend, it's important to understand the difference between saving and investing.

Saving is the act of setting money aside from your income, hopefully in the high-priority, automatic fashion we've been recommending. It's the process of deliberately placing funds into a separate account for future use, whether it's a bank savings account, a money market fund, or a retirement savings plan. *Investing,* on the other hand, is the act of taking the process to the next level. Investing puts your savings to work for growth potentially beyond the minimal interest you would earn if you were to leave your savings alone in a savings account or money market fund.

While it's wise to keep the equivalent of three to six months' expenses in cash or cash equivalents for emergencies (i.e., nonretirement savings accounts or, preferably, money-market funds), keeping *all* of your savings in such conservative accounts will not likely give you the kind of growth you need in order to meet your goals. This is why most financial advisers recommend that a good portion of your *other* (noncontingency-reserve) savings, whether inside or outside of tax-advantaged retirement plans, be invested in equities such as stocks or stock mutual funds.

A quick glance at the history of the U.S. stock market shows us why.

Stocks for the Long Run

The past couple of years have seen stock market corrections and even a "bear market" as a result of several economic forces. These include (1) an overheated economy and its accompanying "irrational exuberance," which drove many stocks to irrationally high prices in relation to their underlying values; (2) an overprotective Federal Reserve, which raised interest rates too high and too swiftly in order to cool the economy's growth—actions that led to a sharp economic and stock market downturn; and (3) the tragic terrorist attacks that temporarily rocked consumer confidence. Equity markets do go up and down in response to world events, economic conditions, and investor sentiment, which is precisely why you do not want to put money into the stock market that you may need within the next five to ten years.

However, a look at the big picture shows that *the stock market is still one of the best places to invest your* long-term *capital*—money that you won't need for the next five to ten years or more.

In 1998, Dr. Jeremy J. Siegel, professor of finance at the Wharton School of the University of Pennsylvania, published a definitive study in which he tracked the return of stocks versus other benchmarks over the preceding 195 years, from 1802 through 1997. This period, of course, included both bull and bear markets as well as the crash of 1929, the ensuing Great Depression, the crash of 1987, and several major market "corrections." Siegel's watershed conclusion, recounted in his book *Stocks for the Long Run* (McGraw-Hill, 1998), is that "over the last century, accumulations in *stocks have always outperformed other financial assets* for the patient investor" (emphasis added).

Let's pretend that your great-great-granddad had $1 to invest from his savings in 1802. He invested for the long run, wanting to pass his dollar and its earnings along to his great-great-grandchild (you). He had five choices: gold, the Consumer Price Index (an investment that keeps pace with inflation), short-term bonds, long-term bonds, or an average stock. What would each investment be worth today? Well, according to Siegel:

- $1 in gold would now be worth $11.17.

- $1 in the Consumer Price Index would be worth $13.37.

- $1 in short-term bonds would be worth $3,679.

- $1 in long-term bonds would be worth $10,744.

- $1 invested in the average stock would be worth $7.47 *million*.

Where do you wish your great-great-granddad had put his dollar? If he had "played it safe" and bought gold, you would inherit $11.17, enough for a big night for two at McDonald's. If he had purchased long-term bonds, you'd probably have close to $10,744, perhaps enough for a modest used car. However, according to Siegel's study, had Great-Great-Granddad bought shares of an average stock, you would likely inherit nearly $7.5 million, enough for . . . well, one can always dream, right?

That's the trend of the U.S. stock market over 195 years. Despite its inevitable ups and downs and a few binges and purges, the market's *long-term* trend has been up—dramatically so.

What about more recent time periods? Consider the following . . .

From 1928 to 1997, which includes the cataclysmic 1929 crash and the Great Depression, the average compounded annual return of the stock market was 11.2 percent. Long-term bonds averaged 5.2 percent.

For the fifty-year period following World War II (1947 to 1997), the average compounded annual return was 12.2 percent, despite the crash of October 1987 and several other corrections. Long-term bonds returned an average of 6.1 percent.

Between 1982 and 1997, a period that included the '87 crash, stocks averaged 16.7 percent; long-term bonds averaged only 8.7 percent.

You May Be Making Stupid Mistake #7 If . . .

- you aren't treating saving for the future as one of your top financial priorities

- you're over age thirty-five and are not saving at least 10 percent of your gross annual income for retirement

- you have a 401(k)- or 403(b)-type plan but are not contributing the full percentage of your salary the plan allows

- you do not have at least a portion of your long-term savings invested for growth in stocks or stock mutual funds (equity investments)

- you've pulled money out of your long-term savings and investments to spend on more immediate things

---

An important caveat is that Siegel's study did not include the enormously profitable years of 1998 and 1999 or, in contrast, the stomach-lurching market sell-offs of more recent years. As we've emphasized, *over the short term,* stocks go up and they go down, and they are not the place to put your contingency or shorter-term savings. But it's heartening to see that over the long haul, equity investments have far surpassed most other common investments, even those that some may consider to be safer. The conclusion we can draw from Siegel's study is that, while there are never any guarantees in the investment world, history gives us good reason to believe that stocks will continue to be a good place for a portion of our long-term money.

We'll look at some easy ways to tap the power of equity investing—and some common mistakes to avoid—in the next chapter.

The Power of Compounding

Now it starts to get fun.

John D. Rockefeller once called compound interest the eighth wonder of the world, and the numbers truly bear him out. With the power of compounding at work, modest sums of money, invested over a period of time, can grow to surprisingly large amounts.

To illustrate, consider the Incredible Game Guy scenario.

A smiling game-show host shows up at your door and shoves a microphone in your face. Behind him, TV cameras record the magic moment. "Congratulations, Mr. and Mrs. Smith," Game Guy begins (which already makes you suspicious because your name isn't Smith). "You have won the grand prize in our Incredible Game Guy contest! You have a choice. You can either take a lump sum of one hundred thousand dollars, or you can take one penny! *What* . . . is your choice?"

It's an easy decision, and besides, you want these people off your porch. "We'll take the hundred thou—" you start to say.

But Game Guy interrupts. "Oh, I forgot to turn my cue card. Your second choice is one penny, doubled each day for thirty days! *What* . . . is your choice?"

Still easy, you reason. One penny doubled equals two cents. Two cents doubled equals four cents. . . . What would the penny option come to? Ten or twenty bucks?

"We'll still take the hundred thou—" you begin again, but your twelve-year-old son, who seems to keep a calculator glued to his palm, interrupts.

"Mom, Dad, *wait.*" He punches in some numbers. *"Take the penny,"* he whispers.

"Son, we know what we're doing," you tell him. But Junior punches the numbers again to verify, then shows you the display. Suddenly you're speechless. You try to speak, but the words just don't come.

So your son says aloud, "We'll take the penny."

Thirty days later, the Incredible Game Guy returns to your door. He hands you a check representing the result of a single penny doubled each day for thirty days. Sure enough, the check is made out for . . . $10,737,418.24.

It sounds incredible, I know. But do the math and you'll find that Junior was right. The secret is *the power of compounding* — not only the eighth wonder of the world, but also your most powerful friend when it comes to building your nest egg. That's because compounding earns you interest not only on the principal you invest, but also *interest on the interest.* Granted, no investor is likely to earn 100 percent daily return on an investment over thirty days. But I share the Incredible Game Guy story to show how even small amounts, invested over time, can grow to almost unbelievable totals through the power of compounding.

For a more real-life scenario, think of Harry, whose parents taught him the wisdom of working with his four powerful friends. Just out of college and starting his career, Harry begins setting aside $100 each month. It's not much, but just you wait. If he puts that money to work in a tax-deferred investment program that averages 12 percent per year (the U.S. stock market average from 1947 through 1997), *and never contributes more than $100 per month* for the rest of his working life, Harry's little $100 monthly savings will be worth $1,176,477 when he reaches sixty-two.

Not too shabby for only $100 per month! Of course, Harry could do far better than that because he's going to increase his monthly savings commitment as his income increases. But his story shows us the incredible power of compound interest over time, given regular top-priority infusions of seed capital — even modest amounts.

To make compounding even more enticing, compare how much Harry will actually contribute from his own pocket with how much of his nest egg will result from compound interest. At $100 per month over the forty years between ages twenty-two and sixty-two, Harry will set aside a total of $48,000 from his income. Thus, of his total $1,176,477 nest egg at age sixty-two, $1,128,477 *is free money* — the result of the power of compounding.

When Friends Work Together . . .

We've introduced your four powerful financial friends. Now let's see how the powers of priority, tax-advantaged saving, equity investing, and compounding can work together to help you build the level of financial independence you desire for your retirement years.

Figure 1 shows the potential growth of the savings you invest in equity investments if those investments average 8 percent annual return, tax-deferred. Figure 2 illustrates a 10 percent average annual return on your investments, and Figure 3 shows what can happen if your investments average 12 percent. Each table illustrates the growth potential of lump-sum contributions, monthly contributions, and annual contributions over various periods of time.

Let's look at Figure 1 for a moment to illustrate the possibilities if your tax-deferred investments average 8 percent annually over time. The "lump sum" section shows that if you presently have $40,000 in a tax-deferred retirement plan, your $40,000 can grow to $86,357 in ten years and to $186,438 in twenty years. The "monthly" section illustrates that having $400 per month automatically transferred to your retirement plan could result in $138,415 in fifteen years and $380,411 in twenty-five years. The "annual" section shows that a $5,000 annual contribution can grow to $247,115 in twenty years and to $611,729 in thirty years.

But those are only examples. Play with the variables in each table by entering your own numbers and totaling the possibilities over ten, fifteen, twenty, twenty-five, and thirty years—depending on how old you are and how many years you foresee working before you shift gears to retirement. You may already have a lump sum working for you in existing retirement plans and hope to continue adding to the plans on a monthly or annual basis. Add the totals and see what happens over different time periods at an 8 percent, 10 percent, and 12 percent average annual compounded return.

By adjusting the lump sums, monthly and annual deposits, length of time for compounding, and projected rates of return, you'll begin to see the incredible potential of the powers of priority, tax-advantaged saving, equity investing, and compounding in reaching your financial goals. With determination and diligence on your part, combined with the help of your four powerful friends, you *can* look forward to a future of financial independence!

Figure 1

8% Annualized Compounded Growth
(Tax-Deferred)

Lump Sum	10 years	15 years	20 years	25 years	30 years
$2,500	5,397	7,930	11,652	17,121	25,157
$5,000	10,795	15,861	23,305	34,242	50,313
$10,000	21, 589	31,722	46,610	68,485	100,627
$20,000	43,179	63,443	93,219	136,970	201,253
$30,000	64,768	95,165	139,829	205,454	301,880
$40,000	86,357	126,887	186,438	273,939	402,506
$50,000	107,946	158,608	233,048	342,424	503,133
$60,000	129,536	190,330	279,657	410,909	603,759
$70,000	151,125	222,052	326,267	479,393	704,386
$80,000	172,714	253,774	372,877	547,878	805,013
$90,000	194,303	285,495	419,486	616,363	905,639
$100,000	215,893	317,217	466,096	684,848	1,006,266
Monthly	10 years	15 years	20 years	25 years	30 years
$200	36,589	69,208	117,804	190,205	298,072
$300	54,884	103,811	176,706	285,308	447,108
$400	73,178	138,415	235,608	380,411	596,144
$500	91,473	173,019	294,510	475,513	745,180
$600	109,768	207,623	353,412	570,616	894,216
$700	128,062	242,227	412,314	665,718	1,043,252
$800	146,357	276,831	471,216	760,821	1,192,288
$900	164,651	311,434	530,118	855,924	1,341,324
$1,000	182,946	346,038	589,020	951,026	1,490,359
Annual	10 years	15 years	20 years	25 years	30 years
$1,000	15,645	29,324	49,423	78,954	122,346
$2,000	31,291	58,649	98,846	157,909	244,692
$4,000	62,582	117,297	197,692	315,818	489,383
$5,000	78,227	146,621	247,115	394,772	611,729
$7,500	117,341	219,932	370,672	592,158	917,594
$10,000	156,455	293,243	494,229	789,544	1,223,459
$15,000	234,682	439,864	741,344	1,184,316	1,835,188
$20,000	312,910	586,486	988,458	1,579,088	2,446,917

Figure 2

10% Annualized Compounded Growth
(Tax-Deferred)

Lump Sum	10 years	15 years	20 years	25 years	30 years
$2,500	6,484	10,443	16,818	27,087	43,624
$5,000	12,969	20,886	33,638	54,174	87,247
$10,000	25,937	41,773	67,275	108,347	174,494
$20,000	51,875	83,545	134,550	216,694	348,988
$30,000	77,812	125,317	201,825	325,041	523,482
$40,000	103,750	167,090	269,100	433,388	697,976
$50,000	129,687	208,862	336,375	541,735	872,470
$60,000	155,625	250,635	403,650	650,082	1,046,964
$70,000	181,562	292,407	470,925	758,429	1,221,458
$80,000	207,499	334,180	538,200	866,776	1,395,952
$90,000	233,437	375,952	605,475	975,124	1,570,446
$100,000	259,374	417,725	672,750	1,083,471	1,744,940
Monthly	10 years	15 years	20 years	25 years	30 years
$200	40,969	82,894	151,874	265,367	452,098
$300	61,453	124,341	227,810	398,050	678,146
$400	81,938	165,788	303,747	530,733	904,195
$500	102,422	207,235	379,684	663,416	1,130,244
$600	122,907	248,682	455,621	796,100	1,356,293
$700	143,391	290,129	531,558	928,783	1,582,342
$800	163,876	331,576	607,495	1,061,467	1,808,390
$900	184,360	373,023	683,432	1,194,150	2,034,439
$1,000	204,845	414,470	759,369	1,326,833	2,260,488
Annual	10 years	15 years	20 years	25 years	30 years
$1,000	17,531	34,950	63,003	108,182	180,943
$2,000	35,062	69,899	126,005	216,364	361,887
$4,000	70,125	139,799	252,010	432,727	723,774
$5,000	87,656	174,749	315,013	540,909	904,717
$7,500	131,484	262,123	472,519	811,363	1,357,076
$10,000	175,312	349,497	630,025	1,081,818	1,809,434
$15,000	262,968	524,246	945,037	1,622,726	2,714,151
$20,000	350,623	698,995	1,260,050	2,163,635	3,618,869

Figure 3

12% Annualized Compounded Growth
(Tax-Deferred)

LUMP SUM	10 years	15 years	20 years	25 years	30 years
$2,500	7,765	13,684	24,116	42,500	74,900
$5,000	15,529	27,368	48,231	85,000	149,800
$10,000	31,058	54,736	96,463	170,001	299,599
$20,000	62,117	109,471	192,926	340,001	599,198
$30,000	93,175	164,207	289,389	510,002	898,798
$40,000	124,234	218,943	385,852	680,003	1,198,397
$50,000	155,292	273,678	482,315	850,003	1,497,996
$60,000	186,351	328,414	578,778	1,020,004	1,797,595
$70,000	217,409	383,150	675,241	1,190,005	2,097,195
$80,000	248,468	437,885	771,703	1,360,005	2,396,393
$90,000	279,526	492,621	868,166	1,530,006	2,696,393
$100,000	310,585	547,357	964,629	1,700,006	2,995,992
MONTHLY	**10 years**	**15 years**	**20 years**	**25 years**	**30 years**
$200	46,008	99,916	197,851	375,769	698,993
$300	69,012	149,874	296,777	563,654	1,048,489
$400	92,015	199,832	395,702	751,539	1,397,986
$500	115,019	249,790	494,628	939,423	1,747,482
$600	138,023	299,748	593,553	1,127,308	2,096,978
$700	161,027	349,706	692,479	1,315,193	2,446,475
$800	184,031	399,664	791,404	1,503,077	2,795,971
$900	207,035	449,622	890,330	1,690,962	3,145,468
$1,000	230,039	499,580	989,255	1,878,847	3,494,964
ANNUAL	**10 years**	**15 years**	**20 years**	**25 years**	**30 years**
$1,000	19,655	41,753	90,345	166,334	300,253
$2,000	42,415	88,980	171,044	315,668	570,545
$4,000	81,724	172,487	332,441	614,336	1,201,010
$5,000	110,696	230,661	442,079	814,670	1,471,303
$7,500	159,833	335,044	643,826	1,188,005	2,147,034
$10,000	196,546	417,533	806,987	1,493,339	2,702,926
$15,000	294,819	626,299	1,210,481	2,240,009	4,054,389
$20,000	393,092	835,066	1,613,975	2,986,679	5,405,852

Extreme Investing

*It's not how much money you make, but what
you do with the money you make.*

After playing with the numbers on the preceding pages, you may be thinking, *Okay, so I need to save more diligently, and I need to put a chunk of those savings to work in equity investments. But the stock market can be risky—look what happened in 2000 and 2001. How do I find an investment that won't keep me awake at night, yet has a chance to average 8 percent, 10 percent, or 12 percent over time?*

Ray felt the same way. In fact, he was so nervous about losing money in the stock market that he kept nearly all of his savings in bank savings accounts and certificates of deposit. While his principal may have been "safer" in these insured accounts, Ray's earnings were limited to between 2 and 5 percent—barely enough to keep up with inflation.

Randy was the opposite of Ray. He not only wanted to see his savings grow, he also wanted them to grow big and fast. So Randy put most of his medium- and long-term savings into technology stocks, including that of the company where he worked. When tech soared in the late 1990s, his portfolio soared, and he felt like a master of the universe. But when tech stocks plunged in 2000 and 2001, Randy's stocks fell nearly 52 percent from their January 2000 highs. He sold his shares near their low point, hoping to avoid further losses.

Ray and Randy illustrate the perils of what I call extreme investing. At one extreme, Ray invests too conservatively. By keeping all his savings in savings accounts and CDs, he will not only battle the ravages of inflation, but he will also fall far short of the rate of growth he needs in order to realize his medium- and long-term goals. If he remains this conservative, Ray will be in danger of outliving his money during his retirement years. He needs to overcome inertia and put his medium- to long-term money to work in equity investments.

At the other extreme is Randy, whose gung-ho, all-eggs-in-one-basket spirit during the late '90s led him to overcommit to one of the higher-risk sectors of the economy. His investments looked great for a time, but the subsequent tech plunge took away not only his earnings but also a chunk of his principal. To top off the carnage, Randy sold his holdings at the worst possible time, when everyone else was selling or had already sold. Instead of "buying low and selling high," he "bought high and sold low," turning his paper losses into actual losses. When and if he feels ready to venture back into the equities markets, he will almost be starting over again. Randy needs to ratchet down his all-or-nothing mentality to a more moderate, diversified approach to investing.

You can readily see why extreme investing is the eighth Stupid Mistake people make with their money: Either extreme gets you nowhere. One gets you nowhere slowly. The other can get you there very fast. Following either Ray's or Randy's example will pose far too great a risk for your financial future.

That's why financial advisers usually recommend a moderate, diversified approach to investing, keeping in mind your particular financial situation and goals, your age, and your tolerance for risk. Because those factors are unique to nearly everyone and because market conditions can change rapidly, I cannot make specific investment recommendations for you—but I can share some important essentials to help keep you away from the extremes . . . and to better prepare you for your own venture into equity investing.

Two Basic Types of Investments

The first thing to keep in mind is that there are two basic types of investments: *debt investments* and *equity investments*. With debt investments you loan money out for interest, while equity investments give you ownership along with its risks and potential rewards.

Debt investments are the more conservative of the two, carrying less risk but also less potential reward. When you purchase a certificate of deposit or a bond, for example, you lend a sum of money to the issuer of that CD or bond for a specified period of time at an agreed-upon rate of return. The certificate or bond you receive is an IOU through which the borrower pledges to pay you the specified interest on a periodic basis, then return the principal amount to you at the end of the term.

On the surface, debt investments appear safer than equity investments. However, keep in mind that their returns are at a fixed rate, usually much lower than the potential return of equity investments over time. It is possible that the entity to which you loan your money could default on the loan or fail to make at least the payments on interest. In many cases, the payback on debt instruments may barely keep pace with inflation or may actually lock you in at a lower rate as current rates move upward. This is why it makes little sense to put an inordinate proportion of your medium- or long-term money in debt investments—especially in your early or midlife years when you have sufficient time to ride out the stock market's inevitable ups and downs.

But debt investments do have their place. As we've seen, money-market funds are excellent places for short-term savings such as your contingency reserve or funds earmarked for other near-term needs. While certificates of deposit and bonds require you to commit your money for specific periods of time (and so are less liquid than savings accounts or money-market funds), they can result in higher earnings. And when it comes to medium- and long-term savings, many investment advisers believe that nearly all of us should keep at least a portion of our savings in debt investments—less when we're younger, more as we grow older— as a hedge against short-term fluctuations in our stock portfolios.

Equity investments, on the other hand, literally give you part ownership in an entity in hopes that the value of that entity will increase over time. For example, when you purchase a home, you hope to build equity—or ownership—in that house. At any given point in time, the current value of the house minus what you owe on the loan equals your equity.

In the stock market, when you purchase stock in a company, you purchase a piece of ownership in that company. If you purchase stock in General Electric, you actually become a part owner of GE. If you invest in a mutual fund that holds shares of Disney, Microsoft, and Procter & Gamble, you become a part owner of those three enterprises, among others. As corporate share values appreciate, your equity grows.

The downside of ownership, of course, is that you also participate in any *declines* in the value of your holdings. As we all saw in recent years, stock prices can go up, and they can go down—sometimes way up or way down. Therefore, equity investments carry higher potential risk than debt investments, and you can indeed lose money in the stock market.

Why, then, should we consider stocks for our long-term savings?

Sleeping with the Equity

The investment world has a mantra that's worth remembering: "Past performance does not guarantee future results." The year 2000 confirmed that mantra as Greenspan's Fed overdosed our red-hot economy with a slew of interest-rate increases. Tech stocks—long priced far above their true value—began to tumble, followed closely by the general stock market. Performance remained dismal for the next two years. Investors with a short-term perspective became discouraged over some significant paper losses in their portfolios. Many even locked in their losses by selling during the downturn.

But those who stayed calm and maintained their long-term perspectives were rewarded for their patience. Even with the market's fall from its historic 1998–99 highs, stocks still showed a gain of an annualized 12.8 percent over the ten years through October 2001. Bonds had gained 7.9 percent. Stocks still won out in the long run.

It's also encouraging to review the bigger picture. Between 1926 and 1999, the U.S. stock market averaged 11.2 percent—despite the crash of '29, the Great Depression, the crash of '87, and numerous other downturns, recessions, and corrections. Between 1994 and 1999, the Standard & Poor's 500 index, which tracks five hundred of the biggest and best stocks, did even better, with average annual returns of more than 26 percent.

Consider, too, a recent study by Ibbotson Associates of Chicago. Over the past sixty years, the study found, an investment in the stock market would have earned you *thirty-two times* what the same amount of money would have earned in certificates of deposit. In other words, for each $10,000 earned in CDs, the stock market has earned $320,000. In addition, over any ten-year period since 1926, stocks have beaten inflation 87 percent of the time while CDs have *under*performed inflation 60 percent of the time.

Stocks go up and stocks go down, but the long-term trend of the U.S. stock market has always been up. Thus, when we invest for a goal that's at least five to ten years away—such as a child's college education or our retirement—we needn't lose sleep over any short-term sell-offs the market may incur. The benchmark we're watching is not the market's performance last week, last month, or even last year; rather, we're watching its performance *over time*. And history is on our side when it comes to long-term equity investing. As Jeremy Siegel concluded in *Stocks for the Long Run*, "Bear [downward] markets, which so frighten investors, pale in the context of the upward thrust of total stock returns. . . . The superiority of stocks to fixed-income investments over the long run is indisputable."

Stock Investing the Easy Way

But if you're like me, you have neither the time nor the desire to spend hours each week poring over charts, prospectuses, and annual reports to choose and manage a portfolio of stocks and bonds. Personally, I'd rather delegate those tasks to professionals who are especially trained for the job and who earn their living by doing the job well.

This is one reason I like *mutual funds* for equity investing. Mutual funds enable anyone to invest in stocks and bonds with the help of full-time, professional fund managers who do all the research and make all the buy-hold-sell decisions. Mutual funds provide diversification across a broad spectrum of companies and industries. We can choose different funds to address different investment objectives. And we can do all of this for an extremely low fee—much lower than we would pay to invest in individual stocks and bonds.

Here's how a mutual fund works. Investors pool their money with a fund manager to buy shares in the fund. The manager invests the money in a selection of stocks, bonds, or other securities, buying and selling according to his or her read on individual companies and overall market trends. The gain or decline in value of the securities held by the mutual fund is averaged at the end of each trading day to determine the fund's daily gain or decline per share as well as its daily price per share. If the fund manager sells a security, investors share the capital gains or losses generated by the sale; if a security owned by the mutual fund declares a dividend, investors also share the dividend.

Instant Diversification

Randy, one of the extreme investors we met at the beginning of this chapter, made the classic mistake of failing to diversify his assets among different types of investments, companies, and industries. As he put nearly all of his money in technology stocks, his go-for-broke attitude almost came true.

Randy was thumbing his nose at an investment principle that dates back nearly three thousand years. Solomon, the wisest and richest ruler the world had ever seen, wrote, "Divide your portion to seven, or even to eight, for you do not know what misfortune may occur on the earth" (Ecclesiastes 11:2 NASB). This time-proven advice recommends *diversification*, the act of spreading the risk among different companies and types of companies so that, if a few should encounter bad fortune, the others can help sustain your principal and (hopefully) your growth.

By their nature, mutual funds help you achieve the diversification you need. Instead of placing all your money in the stock of one company or even three or four companies, mutual funds invest your assets in the stocks of dozens of selected companies. You can diversify your investments further by allocating your money among several different categories of mutual funds such as aggressive-growth, growth, growth-and-income, and international.

There are never any guarantees in the investment business, but diversification helps hedge against potential downslides.

All in the Family

Most mutual funds are part of a mutual fund "family." American Century Investments (800-345-2021, www.americancentury.com), Fidelity Investments (800-544-6666, www.fidelity.com), and The Vanguard Group (800-662-7447, www.vanguard.com) are three popular examples of mutual fund families among dozens to choose from.

A family of funds enables you to diversify your portfolio among different types of funds within the same family and to shift money from fund to fund with one phone call to the family's 800 number. Nearly all families offer taxable and tax-advantaged savings programs through payroll deduction or automatic transfer from personal checking accounts. And most have excellent Web sites with helpful educational tools to help you calculate progress toward your goals and select appropriate mutual funds to help you achieve those goals.

A Fund for Every Investor

Mutual funds have become so popular that there are now more than eight thousand funds to choose from. Regardless of the number of funds, they all fall within three basic types: *stock funds* (equity investments), *bond funds* (short- to long-term debt investments), and *money-market funds* (short-term debt investments). Within the three fund types, you'll find several categories of funds whose portfolio managers invest according to specific objectives. As examples, we'll cite funds from the three mutual fund families listed above: American Century Investments, Fidelity Investments, and The Vanguard Group.

Aggressive-growth funds buy stock in newer or smaller companies that show promising long-term growth potential. They have higher *volatility* (upward and downward swings in changing markets) and higher risk, but higher potential reward. They are best suited for (1) younger investors who have sufficient time to wait out inevitable market ups and downs and to recover from temporary losses and (2) investors who have their other financial bases covered and can afford to devote a slice of their portfolio to higher-risk investments in hopes of higher returns. Examples of aggressive-growth mutual funds include:

- American Century Ultra,

- Fidelity Aggressive Growth,

- Fidelity Capital Appreciation, and

- Vanguard Capital Opportunity.

Growth funds invest in companies that show good growth potential but are usually better established and capitalized than aggressive-growth companies. Volatility and risk for growth funds are moderate to high, depending on the fund and the market, with equivalent reward potential. Almost everyone except older seniors should have a portion of his or her portfolio in growth investments to stay ahead of inflation and to average earnings of 8 percent or better. The proportion allocated to growth can be greater in your early years, then gradually reduced as you grow older. Examples of growth mutual funds are:

- American Century Benham Equity Growth,

- Fidelity Blue Chip Growth,

- Fidelity Growth Company,

- Fidelity Value,

- Vanguard Index Trust 500,

- Vanguard Total Stock Market Index,

- Vanguard/PRIMECAP, and

- Vanguard U.S. Growth.

Growth-and-income funds invest in well-established companies that show potential for continued growth but also spin off income in the form of dividends. These actually did better than many aggressive-growth and growth funds during the bull market of the mid-to-late '90s. Because they invest mostly in blue-chip companies, they carry moderate volatility and risk and moderate reward. You'll want to keep a significant portion of your portfolio in the growth-and-income genre, especially as you grow older. Among the three families we're citing, growth-and-income funds include:

- American Century Equity Income,

- American Century Benham Income & Growth,

- Fidelity Equity-Income II,

- Fidelity Fund,

- Vanguard Equity Income,

- Vanguard Growth & Income, and

- Vanguard Windsor II.

Income funds, or bond funds, invest in more conservative securities such as corporate bonds and U.S. government–backed Treasury bills. They offer low volatility, low-to-moderate risk, and low-to-moderate reward potential. Older retirees whose priority is to preserve capital lean heavily toward income funds. Income funds include:

- Fidelity Capital & Income,

- Vanguard Intermediate-Term Corporate,

- Vanguard Intermediate-Term Treasury,

- Vanguard Short-Term Corporate,

- Vanguard Short-Term Treasury, and

- Vanguard Total Bond Market.

Blended funds take the asset-allocation guesswork from you by combining stocks and bonds in proportions commensurate with the fund's objective. These might also be called balanced funds or asset management funds. They include:

- American Century Balanced,

- Fidelity Asset Manager,

- Fidelity Puritan,

- Vanguard Asset Allocation, and

- Vanguard Wellington.

International funds invest in overseas companies to capitalize on the global economy. Some international funds span the globe; others are specific to regions such as Asia, Europe, and South America. Depending on the stated objectives of a fund, it can invest in overseas companies that fit an aggressive-growth, growth, or growth-and-income profile. Consider these:

- American Century 20th International Growth,

- Fidelity Overseas, and

- Vanguard International Growth.

Sector funds invest in market sectors such as gold mining, health care, banking and finance, real estate, high technology—you name it, there's probably a mutual fund for it. These are less diversified, so they carry greater risk. Health care, for example, has been a strong sector lately because of advances in prescription drugs and in demand for care as people get older. But the health-care sector could show real volatility should the federal government pass cumbersome national health-insurance legislation. Sector funds are like that: They offer good potential with the right timing, but they are susceptible to quick turnarounds. Examples of sector funds are:

- American Century Utilities,

- Fidelity Select Financial Services,

- Vanguard Gold & Precious Metals, and

- Vanguard Health Care.

Index funds are not actively managed by a mutual fund manager because they are computer-driven to hold the same securities followed by various market indices. An S&P 500 fund, for example, owns shares in the same five hundred stocks monitored by the Standard & Poor's 500 index. A fund that follows the Wilshire 5000 index tracks the entire U.S. stock market. There are also bond index funds. Index funds provide an easy way to mirror the overall performance of the markets. Although many fund families are jumping on the index bandwagon, The Vanguard Group originated the concept and continues to lead the field with some of the best funds in the industry:

- Vanguard Index Trust 500,
- Vanguard Total Stock Market Index,
- Vanguard Total Bond Market Index, and
- Vanguard Short-Term Bond Index.

Money-market funds, as we've already seen, invest in conservative, short-term debt instruments such as certificates of deposit, commercial paper, and U.S. government securities. *Outside* of qualified plans, a money-market fund is an ideal place to build your contingency reserve and save for upcoming expenses. *Within* a qualified plan, a money market fund is a good place to park money temporarily while you're deciding which mutual funds to invest in. Among the best money market funds are:

- American Century Prime Money Market,
- Fidelity Cash Reserves, and
- Vanguard Prime Money Market.

The investment objective and other key information for a particular mutual fund are spelled out in a free *prospectus*, which securities law requires fund companies and brokers to offer to anyone considering a mutual fund. You can obtain a prospectus either by calling a company's toll-free number or by downloading it from the fund family's Web site. The prospectus will provide information on the mutual fund's investment objective, sales commissions, expense ratios, investment minimums, fund managers, and historical performance.

Low Cost . . .

You can purchase shares in a mutual fund directly from the mutual fund company, through a discount broker, or through a registered investment adviser. Some funds charge sales commissions ("loads") of anywhere

You May Be Making
Stupid Mistake #8 If . . .

o you're allowing fear to keep you from investing your
long-term savings for growth by means of equity
investments

o more than 10 percent of your long-term savings is
invested in a single stock or industry sector

o you're under age sixty and have less than 50 percent
of your nest egg at work in equity investments

o you're over age forty and have 100 percent of your
nest egg at work in equity investments

o you're any age and don't have a nest egg

o you're investing in a mutual fund with a sales commission or high fees

between 2 and 8.5 percent of your investment, which comes right out of
your principal. Invest $2,000, and the sales commission alone gives you
an instant loss of $40 to $170, which puts you in a catch-up mode from
day one.

The better way is to stick with "no-load" mutual funds, and there are
plenty of excellent ones to choose from. These are usually purchased
directly from the mutual fund company, although more and more registered investment advisers and discount brokers are now offering them.
Invest $2,000, and the full $2,000 goes to work for you. Your money is still
subject to market price swings, of course, but at least you aren't gouged
up-front by a sales commission. The three fund families I've used as
examples in this chapter offer predominantly no-load (in some cases, low-
load) funds.

Don't sign on with any fund that charges the inexcusable *12b-1 fee*, which is actually a smaller *annual* sales load instead of a one-time, up-front charge. Also try to steer clear of the so-called *redemption fee*—a "back-end load" assessed when you sell shares prior to the fund's required holding period—although more and more funds are adding early-redemption fees to discourage short-term, in-and-out trading.

. . . But, of Course, No Free Lunch

As we all know, there's no such thing as a free lunch. To stay in business, mutual funds do assess investors' accounts for the expenses of doing business. These fees are known as *expense ratios* because they're stated as a percentage of dollars invested. When you receive your quarterly statement, the balance shown is your account value after fees have been deducted. Expense ratios are minuscule considering the professional management you get in return.

But when it comes to expense ratios, not all mutual funds are created equal. Some funds spend too much for the results they bring you. So as you evaluate potential funds, keep in mind that ratios for international stock funds should not total more than 1.5 percent of your investment. Domestic stock funds should charge 1 percent or less, with the emphasis on *less*.

The consistent low-fee leader among mutual fund companies is The Vanguard Group; in recent years the average expense ratio for all U.S. funds was approximately 1.31 percent of the amount invested, while Vanguard's averaged 0.27 percent. (For this and other good reasons, Vanguard is one of my favorite mutual fund families.) Lower expenses mean found money to you!

Asset Allocation

What percentage of your medium- and long-term savings should you invest in stock funds? How much in bond or money-market funds? And *what kind* of stock or bond funds?

When it comes to asset allocation, much depends on your tolerance for risk and how soon you'll need to begin drawing from your investments. A conservative rule of thumb suggests that you subtract your age from one hundred; the result is the percentage of your medium- and long-term savings that should be invested in stock funds. (The rest goes to bond and money-market funds.) If you consider yourself moderate to aggressive, willing to place a greater percentage in stocks in hopes of a better return on investment, subtract your age from 125.

Using this approach, Ray, our nervous investor, would subtract his age of forty-two from one hundred to determine that approximately 58 percent of his medium- to long-term savings should be invested in the stock market. This leaves 42 percent to divide between bond and money-market funds.

And Ray doesn't want to spend much time investigating which mutual funds are hot and which are not. To keep life as simple as possible, he's going to use index funds to ensure that his investments keep pace with the overall markets. He'll put his 58 percent stock allotment in a total stock market index fund and divide his 42 percent bond/money-market allotment between a total bond market index fund (35 percent) and a money-market fund (7 percent).

On the other hand, Randy, our more aggressive investor, would prefer to subtract his age from 125. At age thirty-four, this steers 91 percent of his medium- to long-term savings to the stock market and leaves 9 percent for bond and money-market funds. Randy could also choose to use index funds, but he prefers to be more active. He'll divide his 91 percent this way: 30 percent to an aggressive-growth fund, 51 percent to a growth fund, and 10 percent to an international stock fund. He'll place all of his 9 percent bond/money-market fund allotment in a medium-term bond fund.

As you can see, in using this approach both Ray and Randy will gradually reduce their percentage in stocks as they grow older, thereby reducing exposure to risk and helping preserve capital as they draw closer to the time they'll begin using the money.

While investors should always use an approach that enables them to sleep at night, I personally lean toward a more moderately aggressive approach because of its potential to provide a better level of growth and compounding over time. Our goal is to build enough so that we can meet our future goals—the biggest of which is to not outlive our money in our retirement years. In order to stay ahead of inflation, all of us should keep

some of our money invested for growth through equity invest
more in our early years, less in our later years. The following chai
asset-allocation model for retirement-fund investing, is a variation on th
approaches Ray and Randy are using. It suggests potential allocations for
solid growth at different age levels while diversifying assets among various
mutual fund categories. Moderately aggressive in the early years, it gradually becomes more conservative by adjusting the percentage of total assets
one might invest in each category as he or she grows older.

Sample Asset Allocation
for Retirement-Fund Investing

YEARS UNTIL RETIREMENT	STOCK FUNDS	SUGGESTED ALLOCATION	BOND FUNDS	MONEY MARKET FUNDS
30+ years	100%	30%AG, 60%G, 10%INT	0%	0%
20–30 years	95%	25%AG, 60%G, 10%INT	5%M	0%
15–20 years	90%	20%AG, 50%G, 10%GI, 10%INT	10%M	0%
10–15 years	85%	10%AG, 50%G, 15%GI, 10%INT	15%M-S	0%
5–10 years	80%	30%G, 45%GI, 5%INT	15%M-S	5%
0–5 years	70%	10%G, 60%GI	20%S	10%
first 10 years in	60%	60%GI	20%S	20%
next 10 years in	50%	50%GI	25%S	25%
thereafter	40%	40%GI	30%S	30%

STOCK FUNDS:
AG = Aggressive-Growth; G = Growth;
GI = Growth-and-Income; INT = International

BOND FUNDS:
L = Long-Term Maturities (not recommended);
M = Medium-Term Maturities; S = Short-Term Maturities

delines for Investment Success

"paying yourself first" for long-term financial
you're under thirty-five, devote at least 5 percent
of your gross income to long-term (retirement) savings;
from ages thirty-six to forty-five, at least 10 percent; from
ages forty-six to fifty-five, at least 15 percent; and after age
fifty-five, at least 20 percent.

2. *Harness the amazing power of compound interest.* If you
invest just $300 per month in a fund averaging 10 percent
per year, you'll build more than $678,000 over thirty years;
$500 per month grows to more than $1,000,000. The
earlier you start, the better—but it's never too late to
benefit from the power of compounding.

3. *Maximize your tax-advantaged retirement savings plans.*
If your company offers a 401(k) or 403(b) plan, this is your
top priority for long-term savings—especially if your
company matches a portion of your contribution. Once
you've maxed out your company plan for the year, you can
also contribute to Roth or traditional Individual
Retirement Accounts, to SEP-IRAs or Keogh plans if
you're self-employed, and to tax-deferred variable
annuities.

4. *Use mutual funds to simplify your investing.* Mutual
funds help you combine the powers of your four powerful
financial friends: priority, tax-advantaged savings,
compounding, and equity investing. They're managed by
professionals who do all the research and make all the
buy-hold-sell decisions for you.

5. *Use only pure no-load (no sales commission) mutual
funds.* Why pay a salesman a commission of 2 to 8.5
percent of your investment when thousands of high-caliber
mutual funds are available at *no* sales charge? Keep all
your money working for you by sticking with no-loads.

6. *Use low-cost (low expense ratio) funds.* All mutual funds have expense ratios, but some operate far more efficiently than others, which means a lower cost to the shareholders. Pay no more than 1.5 percent for international funds and 1 percent for domestic stock funds. Many excellent funds are available for much less.

7. *Don't chase after the "hot" funds of the day.* Choose funds that have posted good results over three-, five-, and ten-year periods and whose managers have successful track records with the same type of fund over five or more years. Be cautious of all the magazine articles that proclaim, "The 10 Best Funds to Buy Now!"

8. *Diversify among aggressive-growth, growth, and growth-and-income funds through your midlife years.* As you grow older, gradually shift your emphasis toward growth-and-income stock funds combined with a small allotment of bond funds.

9. *To outpace the ravages of inflation, always keep a portion of your assets invested for growth.* You can be more aggressive in your younger years and more conservative as you grow older, but always keep a portion of your portfolio in growth or growth-and-income mutual funds.

10. *Maintain a long-term perspective.* Even with its inevitable ups and downs, the U.S. domestic stock market has averaged an annual return of 11.2 percent since 1926. So don't let temporary downswings frighten or discourage you. Stay strong by maintaining your long-term perspective. Likewise, don't succumb to temptations to withdraw and spend portions of long-term savings—especially your retirement nest egg—until you really need it. Stay the course, and you'll be amazed at the power of your four powerful friends over time.

I want to emphasize that the examples provided in this chapter are by no means the only approaches to asset allocation, nor are they necessarily the best approaches for your situation. Because asset allocation is a highly personal thing, dependent on your age, temperament, goals, and progress to date, I recommend you consult a registered investment adviser, talk to representatives at several mutual fund families or discount brokerages, or, at the very least, log on to some financial Web sites and use the tools provided to help you determine your investment plan. In addition to the mutual fund families cited earlier, I encourage you to contact the following discount brokerages, which provide access to mutual funds from a wide array of mutual fund families. Their phone representatives and Web sites offer helpful answers to your questions and guidance in your investment decisions:

- Charles Schwab & Company, 800-435-4000; www.schwab.com
- Fidelity Brokerage Services, 800-544-9697; www.fidelity.com
- CFSB Direct, 800-825-5723, www.cfsbdirect.com
- TD Waterhouse, 800-934-4448; www.tdwaterhouse.com

Extreme Insurance

*Real life is what happens when you
had other plans.*

Whack!

Tom cried out and dropped the hammer to the floor. In agony, he stifled a few choice expressions of disgust and began massaging his throbbing thumb. He'd better get some ice on it, then wrap it in gauze. It would be black and blue tomorrow, tender to the touch.

Fortunately, Tom had whacked-thumb insurance. He'd seen the dramatic ad on late-night TV, the one with the bad actor lying on the floor and hollering, "I've whacked my thumb and I can't get up!" For the low, low price of just $15.95 per month, Tom had purchased whacked-thumb coverage so in the event of a bashed thumbnail, his medical expenses would be covered. And sure enough, after only three months of claim forms and phone calls, the insurance company, Chester's Casualty and Cheese Logs, reimbursed 100 percent of Tom's medical expenses: 3 cents for the ice and 50 cents for the gauze bandage. Pretty good for just $15.95 a month, huh?

Undoubtedly, you've guessed by now that I'm pulling your leg again. Why? Because it's there. And because sometimes I just can't help myself. The truth is, no credible insurance company offers whacked-thumb insurance—not even Chester's, although the cheese logs aren't bad. And even if someone did offer whacked-thumb insurance, I doubt that anyone bright enough to lift a hammer would be dim enough to spend $191 a year for such coverage.

But it has been known to happen.

I've shared the absurd story of Tom's thumb to help you remember a crucial point about insurance: *The purpose of insurance is to help provide for yourself and/or your family in the face of catastrophic loss, not to reimburse you for every little owie or inconvenience.* To insure against the whacked thumbs of life is to simply pour more money into the money pit than you will ever recoup, even if you were to whack your thumb every day of the year. Better to pay for those small mishaps from your monthly cash flow or your contingency reserve and hold insurance only for the catastrophic losses.

It's never fun to contemplate the big, costly things that could go wrong in life. But that's what financial planning is all about: Determine your goals, put a plan into action, and prepare for contingencies that could sabotage your plan. Good insurance coverage is an essential, helpful part of personal finance. Most of us need insurance in one form or another. However, as with investing, there are extremes to avoid.

At one extreme, some of the best-intentioned among us do not carry essential coverage, exposing our financial future—and that of our loved ones—to serious risk. At the other extreme, some of us, like Tom, are wasting enormous sums of money by purchasing insurance policies, riders, and extras that we don't really need.

So to choose insurance wisely, it's important that we first assess the major areas in which a big surprise could turn into a significant financial crisis. We can't account for every possible catastrophe, but wise insurance coverage for the most common occurrences can keep potentially devastating losses to a minimum. Then we need to be sure we neither *underinsure* (and fall drastically short of the minimum provision needed) nor *overinsure* (and waste hundreds or even thousands of premium dollars for insurance we really do not need).

Insurance You Probably Need—But Not Always

In Chapter 4 we considered some important basics to keep in mind when shopping for auto insurance. Now let's consider other key areas of your financial life: why insurance coverage may be necessary for your situation, what to look for in a good policy, and potential sources of good insurance values. Then we'll review several other popular insurance coverages that you most likely do *not* need; discarding and avoiding them could save you hundreds of dollars each year, money that can be more wisely utilized in shoring up your *necessary* insurance coverage or in your investment program.

Life Insurance

The fundamental question to ask yourself when it comes to life insurance is *Who, if anyone, depends on my present and future stream of income?*

The purpose of life insurance is to replace your income for dependents who would otherwise suffer significant financial hardship upon your death, for as long as they reasonably expect to remain dependent. Thus, you want life insurance to assure your spouse the annual cash flow he or she will need indefinitely and to provide for your children until (and only until) they reach the age of independence. Whether you're a primary, secondary, or equal breadwinner, you need life insurance if any of the following is true:

- your spouse and/or family depends on your income for everyday needs including food, clothing, transportation, and shelter;

- they need your earnings to help eliminate debt;

- you're planning to use a portion or all of your income in future years to pay most of your children's college expenses;

- you and your spouse are counting on several years' additional income from you to provide for retirement.

The amount of life insurance you need (called *face amount*) depends on your debt, liquid assets, number and ages of children, what you have your heart set on providing, and the number of years your children and spouse would need to compensate for the cutoff of your income. The idea is to provide a lump sum large enough for your surviving spouse to (1) invest at a moderate return and (2) draw from those earnings as needed while leaving the principal untouched until later in life.

Taking into account your present level of savings and investments, your debt structure, and your present living expenses, *aim for a face amount of approximately $100,000 for every $500 in monthly expenses your spouse would need to replace.* The sum may appear huge, but it's a necessity if you have dependents and do not have several hundred thousand in liquid funds to provide for them in your absence.

Getting the face amount you need is easier, though, when you shop for the *right kind* of life insurance. *Term* insurance can buy you five to ten times the face amount of so-called *permanent* (a.k.a. "whole life") insurance, which combines insurance coverage with an expensive, low-yield "cash value" account. *Decreasing term* holds its premium level while gradually decreasing its face amount benefit. *Annual renewable term* holds its face amount but increases your premium every year. The policy to look for is *level-premium term,* which locks in both the face amount benefit as well as your premium level for the life of the policy.

You'll find the best deals through an independent broker who specializes in monitoring an array of companies for the best policies and prices. Some good ones include Direct Insurance Services (800-622-3699), MasterQuote (800-337-5433), and SelectQuote (800-343-1985). You can also find brokers online (including www.quicken.com/insurance and www.allquoteinsurance.com).

(It's important to remember that you should never cancel an existing policy until you have been fully accepted by a new company with a better policy. You don't want to be caught "between insurance" or, worse, be denied new coverage after you've canceled an existing policy.)

Health Insurance

If your workplace offers a health plan, that's usually the most cost-effective way to go. If you're self-employed or in another situation in which you need private medical insurance, you'll quickly find that medical insurance is some of the costliest stuff around—but that doesn't make it any less necessary.

Check your yellow pages for independent brokers who specialize in personal medical insurance coverage. In addition to information on major medical plans, ask for information on Medical Savings Accounts, which allow you to set aside a specified dollar amount each month on a pretax basis and choose your own medical providers. Also check insurance Web sites such as www.ehealthinsurance.com and www.allquotesinsurance.com, which allow you to play with plan variables and receive quotes on the spot.

As you evaluate possibilities, keep in mind that you want to cover potentially catastrophic expenses but not every little medical contingency such as Tom's thumb. Keep your premiums lower by choosing higher deductibles and copayments.

Disability-Income Insurance

If you were disabled by illness or injury and unable to earn a paycheck for several months or years, how would your family fare? Some financial experts call serious disability a "living death" because, while the victim can no longer provide an income, he remains alive and thus cannot leave a life-insurance death benefit to his dependents. In fact, he becomes a dependent himself, requiring food, clothing, shelter, and possibly expensive equipment and ongoing medical, rehabilitative, or nursing care. It's a crisis more common than we like to contemplate.

The purpose of disability-income insurance is to provide income replacement in the event of a long-term, debilitating illness or injury. Typically, disability income insurance will replace up to 60 percent of your gross income.

As with major medical insurance, the most cost-effective way to attain coverage is through a group plan if your employer offers one. However, many companies do not offer disability, and the self-employed are also on their own. It's insurance I hope you will never need to use, but in the event of a long-term problem, you'll be grateful you made the investment.

Look for the following features:

Definition of disability. Accept a policy only if it defines disability as being unable to do the work you usually do. This is called the *own occupation* definition, as opposed to *any occupation*. Why is this important? Well, "any occupation" policies define disability as being unable to work in *any* occupation. Technically, as soon as you're able to say, "Would you like fries with that?" the insurance company considers you able to work and can terminate benefits. See why you want the policy to come through if you're unable to work at your *own occupation*?

Benefit duration. This refers to the number of years you want benefits to be paid. The longer the duration of benefit, the higher the premium. You can designate as little as two years, but I suggest a minimum duration of five years since many disabling conditions clear up adequately to return to work within that period of time. You can specify up to age sixty-five to insure against a permanent disability.

Waiting period. A *waiting period* is the equivalent of the deductible for auto, homeowners, and medical insurance—it's the time between determination of disability and when benefits begin. The longer the waiting period, the lower your premium, and providers typically let you choose a waiting period of thirty days to a year. If you can, opt for a waiting period of three to six months for better premium value—but only if your contingency reserve is built up to three to six months' living expenses to cover you during the wait.

Noncancelable and guaranteed renewable. If a prospective policy requires ongoing medical exams, it most likely can be canceled at the insurer's discretion. Be sure yours specifies that it's noncancelable and guaranteed renewable.

Residuals and COLAs. As you're making your comeback from a disability, your doctor may advise you to ease back into your work schedule—maybe half days or three days a week until you're back to your usual fit 'n' feisty self. A *residual benefit* ensures that you're paid a partial benefit to compensate for the time you're still unable to work. Since many disabilities play out this way, a residual benefit is worth having. A *cost-of-living-adjustment* (COLA) will automatically keep your benefit apace with inflation.

Try these sources for personal disability-insurance plans: Direct Insurance Services (800-531-8000) and Wholesale Insurance Network (800-808-5810), www.allquotesinsurance.com, www.DisabilityInsurance.net, and www. Disability-Insurance-Center.com.

Homeowners or Renters Insurance

If you're a homeowner with a mortgage, your lender requires you to carry adequate homeowners insurance to protect "his" investment. Homeowners insurance typically wraps three types of coverage into one: *your dwelling, your personal property,* and *potential liabilities* arising from the fact that you're a property owner. As with most insurance, the higher the deductible, the lower your premium, so insure against catastrophe instead of the small stuff. Maintain adequate savings in your contingency reserve to pay deductibles and small claims yourself. Be sure these key coverages are part of your policy:

You May Be Making Stupid Mistake #9 If . . .

o you've purchased life insurance on your children

o you've purchased credit life or mortgage life insurance

o you're a key provider for your family and don't have disability income insurance

o you've purchased permanent life insurance (a.k.a. "whole life") instead of term life insurance

o you're trying to cover every contingency with insurance

Full replacement coverage. It used to be that insurance companies offered a provision guaranteeing "full replacement value" of your home, even if the home's value increases far beyond the amount of insurance in force. But then insurers realized this might cost them some money, so they shifted the burden back to you. Check your homeowners policy every two years to be sure your current replacement coverage would indeed replace your home at today's cost. An inflation rider can help your policy keep up with the times.

Flood insurance. Homeowners policies typically cover water damage resulting from ruptured pipes or water heaters, but no private insurer wants to cover damage due to flooding from outside sources (which tells you something about how big a risk flood damage must be). If you live near a body of water or a river or a canyon . . . if your home is in a low-lying area that would collect water in a major deluge . . . if basements in your neighborhood are subject to water seepage . . . and particularly if your county has designated your neighborhood a flood plain, then you should take steps to fill this gaping hole in your homeowners policy.

As I've stated, your private insurer doesn't want to touch this hazard. Fortunately, the federal government stands ready to help with its reasonably priced National Flood Insurance Program. Your insurance agent or broker can supply informational brochures, or you can call the National Flood Insurance Program directly at 800-638-6620.

Personal property and liability. Personal property is all the stuff you keep inside the house. Usually this coverage is a given percentage of the dwelling coverage. You can purchase optional riders for specific items of value if you like. *Liability* coverage protects you against lawsuits arising from awful things that might happen to others while they're on your property. Carry coverage of at least $100,000 per occurrence.

If you rent a home or apartment, your landlord is responsible for dwelling coverage. However, you still need personal property and liability coverage, both readily available in the form of *renters insurance.* You can buy good policies from the same insurers that provide homeowners coverage.

Homeowners and renters insurance premiums vary widely for comparable benefits, so comparison-shop at least three companies. AAA, American Family, Allstate, and GEICO are good places to start looking.

Liability Insurance

We live in a world where anything that goes wrong is always someone else's fault. Especially if there's money to be made by placing blame.

A lady holding hot coffee in her lap as she drives hits a bump and spills the coffee all over herself. She sues the restaurant where she bought the coffee . . . and wins.

A helmetless boy from the neighborhood skateboards into your driveway, tumbles to the concrete, and breaks his nose. His parents sue you for negligence and child endangerment, despite the fact that their little angel was trespassing and that the broken nose may actually be an improvement.

We live in a sue-happy society. If Santa slides off your roof and busts his tailbone, he could sue you, and probably will.

Daytime TV runs countless ads featuring Larry the Lawyer loudly admonishing us to sue whoever may be causing us real or perceived pain ("Larry got me my check!"). If all the lawyers in our country were placed end to end, it would be a good start. But until that blessed day, we're left to contemplate all the silly things for which people sue people, recognizing that the next victims of lawsuit larceny could be *us*.

We've briefly considered the basic liability coverage provided by your homeowners (or renters) insurance and your auto insurance. These are the necessary starting points of good liability coverage. But are they enough?

As long as Larry the Lawyer is alive and well, probably not.

That's where *excess liability insurance* comes in. Excess liability insurance is more casually known as an *umbrella policy* because it provides coverage for just about any kind of personal judgment or settlement not directly related to your employment. It's called excess liability insurance because it kicks in once your homeowners/renters or auto liability coverage has been exhausted. You can carry $1 million in coverage for just a few hundred dollars per year—a bargain few of us should pass up. Another nice benefit of umbrella insurance is that the insurer will most likely provide you with rigorous legal counsel because he doesn't want to pay a judgment any more than you do.

To take advantage of multiple-policy discounts, purchase umbrella insurance from the same provider that insures your auto and residence.

Long-Term Care Insurance

What if a traffic accident, a fall from a ladder, or an early stroke were to require you or your spouse to stay in a custodial-care facility for several months? When you think about it, there aren't many risks that could drain one's financial reserves faster than a lengthy stay in a long-term care facility. And as we move through adulthood toward our retirement years, we draw ever closer to the age at which 40 percent of Americans indeed spend some expensive time in nursing homes.

More and more companies are wisely including long-term care insurance as part of their benefits packages. If yours does not, consider lining up private long-term-care insurance after age fifty. The older you are when you buy, the higher your premium—but once you buy in, your premium stays level for as long as you own the policy. (Providers remain entitled to make across-the-board premium increases, such as for every policyholder within a certain state or region.)

Here are some important elements to watch for as you shop for long-term care policies:

Provider stability. If you start buying long-term care coverage in your fifties, you want it to be there for you in your eighties. Therefore it's important that your insurer doesn't decide to fold up his tent down the road. (Unfortunately, after experimenting with long-term care products, a few have done just that and retreated from the long-term care business.) As you shop, consider a provider only if it demonstrates two vital qualifications: (1) It has been dealing in long-term care insurance for at least ten years, and (2) it is highly rated for fiscal strength by independent watchdogs A.M. Best (908-439-2200), Moody's (212-553-0377), and Standard & Poor's (212-208-8000).

Qualification for benefits. Most policies require medical confirmation that your situation arises from one of three conditions: (1) medical necessity, (2) cognitive impairment, or (3) the inability to carry out fundamental activities of daily living. Don't accept a policy that allows the insurance company's hired guns to make that determination. Insist that such confirmation be made by *your* physician.

Duration of benefits. Much like a disability-income policy, the *benefit period* is the length of time your policy will pay out per nursing home stay. Since the average stay is almost three years, this should probably be the *minimum* benefit period you consider. Unfortunately, many nursing home stays are longer—even for the duration of your life. If your current and future cash flow allows, *lifetime* is the ideal choice.

Elimination period. As with disability income, long-term care coverage also gives you a choice of how long you'll pay your own way before benefits kick in. Weigh your contingency reserve and other liquid assets against the fact that the average nursing-home stay costs approximately $3,500 per month. The longer the elimination period, the lower your premium.

Inflation rider. Especially if you purchase long-term care coverage in your fifties, you'll want to include the inflation rider to allow for the upward creep of prices. Look for policies offering an inflation benefit of 4 to 5 percent per year.

Start your research into long-term care insurance by contacting brokers for information and comparative quotes. Check Bisys Long-Term Care Marketing Group (800-678-4582) and Long-Term Care Quote (800-587-3279). Also check www.longtermcarewiz.com, www.LTCinsurance.com, and www.1stlongtermcare.com.

Insurance You Probably Don't Need

The following types of insurance are sources of big money for insurers because, in reality, claims are rarely made on these policies—or they carry sufficient fine print to protect the insurer from significant liability. High profitability and low liability may explain why you receive mail and phone pitches for such coverage nearly every week.

Credit Life Insurance

Credit card companies do everything they can to get you to run your credit to stratospheric levels; then they play the guilt card: Sign up for credit life insurance to "protect your loved ones" by paying off your consumer debts "in case something happens to you." (*Now* they care about your financial stewardship.) You'll come out much better if you just add any consumer debt to your calculations when you buy your regular term life insurance coverage. Better yet, stay debt-free and make credit life insurance completely irrelevant.

Mortgage Life Insurance

Before you moved the last box from the moving van to your new living room, your lender and every other mortgage company in the universe began filling your mailbox with letters encouraging you to "make sure your loved ones are provided for" with mortgage life insurance that will pay off your mortgage if you die. But the math quickly reveals that these products are rarely a good value. If it's important to you to leave a paid-in-full home to your spouse and family, figure the outstanding mortgage into your calculations when purchasing your own level-term life insurance policy.

Life Insurance on Your Kids

"If you love your kids, you'll of course want to carry life insurance on them." This line, a favorite among life insurance sales folk, leaves their brains at the door. The purpose of life insurance is to help replace lost income in the event of the death of a key income provider. Children are rarely the family breadwinners, so why cover them with life insurance? It makes little sense, except to the insurance agent who pockets the commission.

Life Insurance for Singles with No Dependents

The same principle applies here. Who will suffer from the loss of your income if you die? If no one depends on you for income, life insurance is unnecessary.

Flight Insurance

If you're properly covered with your own life insurance policy, don't let fear or guilt compel you to purchase more just as you're heading to the departure gate. Statistically, even in today's nervous environment, flying is still the safest form of transportation—and if you've designed your level-term life insurance program properly, your loved ones will be adequately provided for should the unthinkable happen.

Dread-Disease Insurance

What possible financial difference does it make *how* you die? The amount of life insurance you need to provide for your loved ones is not determined by *how* you leave the earth, but by the simple fact that you leave. Again, your level-term life insurance should be adequate.

TV Life Insurance

Forget the TV sales pitches from celebrities offering life insurance for "only $10 per unit," with no medical exam needed. Notice they don't specify what they mean by "unit." Could be $10 per month per $1,000 face amount. Take a calculator to it, and you'll see how they afford all those TV ads in the first place.

Accidental Death Insurance

Do you really want to be worth more if you die by accident than if you die by natural causes? Your loved ones should never have to depend on you to die in a specific way. Again, there's little logic (but much profit) to this rider that insurance agents love to add to insurance applications "for just a few dollars more." If the face amount of your policy is what it needs to be, then you or your loved ones won't have to worry about making your death look like an accident.

Towing and Car-Rental Reimbursement Riders

Forget riders to your auto insurance policy covering towing and car-rental reimbursement. You'll do better on those with a AAA membership—minus the hassle of filing a claim.

Credit Card Protection Insurance

Here's another favorite of credit card companies: For a few dollars a month you can register all your credit cards with their "guardian" (or similar moniker) program, and in the event your cards are lost or stolen, they'll place a stop-loss on your cards to protect you from having to pay for a bad guy's wild spending spree. The fact is, the law already protects you from any fraudulent use of your credit card beyond $50. Besides, if you're steering clear of Stupid Mistake #5, you're now down to just one credit card, right? You may even be keeping it safe in your freezer or your safe deposit box. If you keep good records and stay vigilant, credit card protection insurance is unnecessary.

Extended Warranties

Purchase any appliance today, and you'll be pitched an *extended warranty* promising service or replacement if the appliance dies following its manufacturer's warranty. And if you don't buy the coverage on the spot, you're destined to receive multiple phone calls and letters repeating the opportunity. Extended warranties may sound good on the surface, but ask yourself this question: *Why are they offering to help me in this way?* It's because the odds are strongly in the insurer's favor that he'll never have to make good on his offer and your extra premium dollars can go straight to his daughter's orthodontist. Yes, appliances do go kaput occasionally, but not often enough to shift the odds in your favor. You'll usually come out ahead if you skip extended warranties.

To Avoid Extreme Insurance . . .

When it comes to insurance, there's a wise middle ground between extremes. Don't get caught *underinsured* against potentially devastating events. Some prudent premium dollars now can guard against the loss of hundreds of thousands down the road. At the same time, don't *overinsure* and waste big money covering relatively minor risks. You can pay for whacked thumbs yourself.

Teaching Stupid Mistakes
to the Next Generation

*Our parents tried to convince us that money
doesn't grow on trees. Now we have to convince
our kids that money doesn't come from ATMs.*

If there's anything worse than making one of the 12 Stupid Mistakes ourselves, it's got to be enabling these miscues in our children and grandchildren.

It's tough enough to manage our own lot, get through life in one piece, stay fiscally solvent, do some good, and leave a positive legacy. But for many adults, another big part of life is the challenge of parenthood. It takes money to rear children. It also requires wisdom (and concerted effort) to teach them financial reality, responsibility, and independence.

Young children, for example, may have a hard time understanding that the ATM doesn't print unlimited handfuls of money for us whenever we want it. And it doesn't take kids long to start asking, whining, fussing, and crying for anything in a store checkout lane that appeals to them. Children are born with a priority inversion: They want what they see, and they want it now. Their young minds are not programmed for discernment or financial accountability. They don't readily understand that someone had to work hard for the money that slides out of the machine and pays for the candy.

They also watch us like hawks, especially as they grow older. Although they'll roll their eyes and deny it, they observe what we do, file it away in their I'll-Never-Do-That-to-My-Kids file, then proceed to do those very things themselves. So if we make foolish financial mistakes, chances are they'll duplicate our errors somewhere down the road.

The Book of Proverbs records an important admonition for parents: "Train a child in the way he should go, and when he is old he will not turn from it" (Proverbs 22:6 NIV). When you think about it, this is exactly what all loving parents try to do: train their children to do right, be responsible, be productive, and care for others. In that light, I'm convinced that one of the most significant gifts we can bestow upon our children is a sense of financial responsibility and independence. Since money is a tool for living life, it follows that one of our most meaningful legacies could be making sure our kids learn to use that tool wisely—for their good and for ours.

When our kids leave the nest, won't it be reassuring to know that, among the other values we've sought to teach them, they have the determination and the skills to make it on their own? that they understand the importance of hard work and the value of a dollar? that they share your priorities of giving, saving and investing, and wise purchasing decisions?

But in order to impart this gift to them, we must begin early to teach and model some pivotal realities about money:

- Money comes from hard work, not from ATMs.

- It comes in limited—not endless—quantities.

- For everything they want to buy, we must exchange a portion of that limited quantity of hard-earned money.

- If we do not buy them everything they want, they will not die.

Unlike what generations of parents have tried to do with the birds and bees, these realities cannot be taught in one-time lectures. They need to be conveyed from our children's toddler years through their young adulthood, reinforced with steadfastness in the face of demands, and modeled by the way in which we handle *our* money.

Enabling Entitlement

The easy out, of course, is to throw money at this challenge by simply giving our children the money or things they want. We've all watched our friends or families make this mistake. It's an unfortunate trend.

We do not set out to ruin our kids, and our kids don't set out to be ruined. Intentions are usually honorable. But look around and see if you don't agree: In order to be considered good providers, demonstrate our love, make up for lost "together time," or keep the peace, too many of us are supplying our children with just about everything kids are convinced they must have.

Their own cell phones.

Their own cars.

Their own TV sets in their own bedrooms.

Their own computers.

The hot new computer games.

The CD Walkman with earphones.

The peer-approved clothing.

The $120 designer sneakers.

Bigger allowances.

Their own credit cards.

In our hearts, we may sincerely believe that this is what good parents do. We don't want our children to feel the cruel rejection of their peers or the awkwardness of being the only person without. We care. We want to provide what they need. Unfortunately, some of us have let our good intentions get out of hand. Perhaps we became too preoccupied, too pressured by our jobs, or too tired to take full advantage of some teachable moments. Maybe it was easier to choose the path of least resistance.

On the other hand, we may be struggling with our own priority inversion. Perhaps we've spent and acquired so much for ourselves that we're enslaved by the monster. As we scramble to sustain the ravenous beast, possibly longing for our own illusive Someday to bail us out, we are being watched . . . by our children. Whether we realize it or not, we are modeling financial values and attitudes. We will likely be emulated. We teach more by what we do than by what we say.

Regardless of the whys or the hows, and despite our best intentions, many of us have enabled a spirit of entitlement in our children.

You May Be Making
Stupid Mistake #10 If . . .

o you give in to your toddler's demands in a grocery store checkout lane

o you tend to give your child money and things instead of your time

o you'd rather be your child's friend than his parent

o you frequently give your child extra money after he's spent his allowance

o you do not require your child to give and save a portion of every dollar she earns

o your adult child is still living with you

o you tend to scrimp in your senior years in order to leave an inheritance

What do I mean by *enabling entitlement?*

To *enable* means to "make able," to supply with the means and opportunity, to encourage. To *entitle* is to grant legal or moral right to something. Thus, to *enable entitlement* is to encourage and facilitate a sense that one has the right to whatever he or she may desire to do or possess.

We've seen this phenomenon in government assistance programs, which are often referred to as *entitlements.* Originally conceived to provide temporary, safety-net assistance to people in dire need, many of these programs have mushroomed out of control. Why? Because in many cases, these programs inadvertently taught a vast population to literally *expect* such assistance to continue the rest of their lives. It's not bad people, just human nature. They received the money, they grew accustomed to getting it, and therefore they now feel they have a right to it. They're entitled.

In much the same way, many of us accidentally foster a sense of right and entitlement among our own children. It may have started in that checkout lane years ago, when we acquiesced to our toddlers' extortion attempts. As they grew older, maybe we simply made too much stuff too available too easily, without slowing down and giving them what they *really* wanted: our time. More often than we'd like to admit, we gave them things instead of giving them ourselves.

Too quickly, they went into middle school and then high school. Shaky identities and peer pressure moved in, big time. When their friends bought the latest fad, our kids felt they had a right to it as well. The new GAMECUBE is cool, and they're entitled to be cool. If we don't allow or supply it, there could be pouting. Even rebellion. We don't want pouting or rebellion; we want to be our kids' friends.

Paying the Price

Some well-meaning parents keep the pattern going—even after their nest is supposedly empty. They may keep paying big bucks for a child's endless college education while he continually switches majors or takes sabbaticals to "find himself." Time and again, these parents will run to the financial aid of an adult child if she gets into a jam or give her money if she wants something she cannot afford on her own.

These kindhearted parents may allow a listless adult child to move back into their home and sponge from them indefinitely, depleting their cupboards and their cash flow. Family counselors David and Claudia Arp have stated that more than one-third of unmarried American men between the ages of twenty-five and thirty-four still live at home with their parents. And more and more young adult daughters are moving back into the empty nest—with a child or two for Grandma or Granddad to care for.

It goes without saying (but I'll say it anyway) that the dependent adult-child is also likely to count on, long for, and feel he has a right to his ultimate entitlement: an inheritance. That illusive Someday will finally arrive, he thinks, and he'll finally be home free.

No, we never intended to foster entitlement. But it's happening in many families, and it's a gross disservice to our children. Too many of our kids have learned instant gratification instead of delayed gratification, debt-laden consumerism instead of debt-free liberty. Too many have begun looking for someone else to pay their way instead of reaching for healthy self-reliance. Too many have embraced the spirit of entitlement instead of the reality of hard work and tough choices.

Stemming the Tide

Granted, no matter how conscientious we are as we try to raise responsible children, God created them with free will. Even if we do everything right— something no human parent has achieved yet—our kids may still choose weak values or make poor decisions. However, we *can* redouble our resolve to do our part as parents to "train a child in the way he should go." For our children's sake, we can begin to stem this tide of dependence and entitlement by first reconnecting with the values we want our kids to observe in us—values that emerge from the wreckage of the 12 Stupid Mistakes:

- The future is now, not Someday.

- Financial independence is up to *you*—not your parents, your employer, your government, or your adult children.

- Rainy days are inevitable. Prepare for them.

- You are not what you can buy.

- Money doesn't grow on trees, nor does it come from ATMs. Someone works hard for it.

- You are not what you drive.

- If you can't afford to pay for it today, you can't afford to pay for it with interest tomorrow. If it's worth having, it's worth waiting for.

- Take good care of your health.

- Make giving, saving, and investing your most important financial priorities.

- Learn to use your four powerful friends: priority, tax-advantaged saving, equity investing, and compounding.

- Avoid extremes in investing and insurance.

- Keep your records in order.

- If you're in your thirties or older, make retirement savings your top financial priority.

- Make the most of what you have . . . to make the most of the rest of your life.

Re-embracing these principles in our own lives will help us model sound financial doctrine for our children as they grow older and strike out on their own.

Money and Tough Love

In parenting, tough love draws the line for children and then stands firm whenever they challenge that line. In our financial parenting, I believe it's time for tough love. Time to draw the line, define the boundaries, and stand strong when challenged. And we *will* be challenged. If we give in or fudge, we teach entitlement. When we remain steadfast, we teach responsibility.

Financial parenting could be the subject of a book unto itself, so let me recommend a good one to get you started: *Money-Savvy Kids* by J. Raymond Albrektson (WaterBrook Press, 2001). Albrektson shares the values and tactics that worked for him and his wife as they raised two children, both of whom are now responsible, productive adults.

Meanwhile, I'll leave you with some tough-love suggestions to help you guide your kids away from entitlement and toward financial responsibility. (Is it coincidence that there are *twelve* of them?)

1. In store aisles and checkout lanes with young children, just say no.

2. Begin early giving your children modest allowances, and gradually increase the amounts as they grow older. Consider requiring your kids to (a) give 10 percent to the church offering or to a charity they help choose, (b) save at least 20 percent, and (c) spend the rest at their leisure or save it for a future purchase.

3. Don't make the common mistake of linking allowances with the performance of household chores. Children should be expected to do chores solely because they are members of the family. If they link their allowances with household responsibilities, the next time you ask them to do something they may expect payment for it.

4. If children spend their allowances and pout for more, don't dip into your wallet to supplement their spending. That teaches entitlement, not stewardship. Use such moments to reinforce that spending has a price; they must wait until the next regular allowance.

5. Teach the importance (and the extra measure of joy) of *delayed gratification*. If they have their eye on something they want, encourage them to save for it and purchase it with their own money.

6. As children grow older, encourage part-time work on weekends or during summers. A smart friend of mine not only encouraged his growing kids to find part-time jobs, but he also required them to give 10 percent of their earnings to their church and to save 50 percent for college. They learned the priority of giving by actually doing it from day one. When college time came, they experienced a tremendous shot of self-reliance because they were able to pay a major portion of their college expenses themselves.

7. Think carefully about buying, or allowing teenage children to buy, their own cars. Those dollars could be put to much better use for their futures. But if you're inclined to approve, help your children learn to count the cost ahead of time by totaling the cost of payments, registration, insurance, gas, oil, and maintenance. Better yet, require children to pay most or all of these costs themselves—from the *spendable* portion of their allowances or part-time earnings. (The giving and saving portions should remain sacred.)

8. Begin saving early for your children's college education through tax-advantaged plans such as Section 529 plans and Education Savings Accounts (ESAs, formerly Education IRAs). Consider the value of having your children work part time, from middle school through their college years, to fund as much of their education as they can.

9. To encourage diligence and to discourage endless education or sabbaticals from college, consider putting a cap on the financing of your children's college education. When your child is in middle school or early high school, you might say, "We will partner with you in paying for college. You apply all of your college savings, and we'll pay the difference— for four years or your first degree, whichever comes first. Anything after that is up to you."

10. Once children are on their own, stay emotionally and spiritually supportive but be slow to jump in with financial bailouts. They must learn

to fly on their own, and this may involve making their own mistakes or working through their own tough times. When you see a child struggling, or if he hints or asks for money, consider three questions: *Is this a genuine crisis or only a temporary inconvenience? What's the worst that can happen if I do not give him money? What will I be teaching him if I do?*

11. If an adult child is in a jam and the only compassionate solution is to let him move in with you, be firm in establishing your ground rules up-front. It's your house, and he is your houseguest. Some parents in this situation have reduced stress by setting a deadline and making their expectations clear *prior to* giving their consent: "The limit is _____ weeks. We expect you to be back on your feet and out on your own by then. While you are here, you will (a) be up by 7 each morning and in by midnight each night, (b) aggressively search for a job, (c) contribute _____ dollars each week toward room and board, and/or (d) help us (name chores) around the house."

12. In Chapter 1, I shared why I believe it's inappropriate to plan on a financial inheritance from our parents—to behave as if we are entitled to it. Whatever financial resources our folks have set aside are for *them,* not for us. Our parents have already given us all we need and more than we can ever repay. They should feel no further pressure or obligation to scrimp or forgo their own dreams in order to conserve their estate for us. We're adults now. We're on our own. Model this spirit for your children by encouraging your aging parents to live out their dreams.

And we should also free ourselves of the same self-imposed pressure. Our children observe (and learn from) our attitudes toward our parents' money. If they see any indication that we expect or count on an inheritance, they will quite naturally assume that they are entitled to the same from us. Sure, we're morally obliged to leave our kids a legacy of love, provision, nurture, character, and a name they can be proud of—but there is no moral or legal ordinance requiring that we leave children a substantial financial inheritance. In many cases, leaving a large chunk of money would be the worst possible thing we could do for them.

When you are in your retirement years, your chief financial concern will be making your money last as long as you do. Don't shortchange yourself by considering some of your retirement money untouchable because it's "for the kids." That money is yours, not theirs. Your true legacy will be the values you've taught your children. You reared them with all the love and wisdom you could muster. You shoved them gently from the nest; now they must fly. They're on their own. If you spend your last nickel on your last day but leave a legacy of love, you will have done your job well.

If you should end up leaving a financial inheritance at journey's end, that's wonderful! Just don't scrimp through your retirement years in order to do so. Don't turn away opportunities for personal growth, out-reach, and adventure just so you'll have more to pass along. Let God determine whether your kids receive a financial inheritance and, if so, how much. They already have your true legacy to treasure. Money is only icing on the cake.

Financial Clutter

The long period of adjustment after a loved one's death is often complicated by issues concerning money. Sometimes the person who has died has failed to plan ahead. Sometimes those left behind do not understand how to go forward financially.

—SUZE ORMAN, *The Road to Wealth*

We don't have a financial file. We have a financial *pile*."

Tim, a financial planning client, laughed as he said it, and I joined in. "I can *use* that," I said, thinking of future writing and speaking projects. I assured Tim that he and his wife, Laurie, were not atypical—that many, if not most, adults have not taken the time to organize their financial records for easy access.

Keeping organized, up-to-date financial records is not exactly an exciting subject, I know. It's about as enthralling as watching paint dry, and I realize that it is not the key reason you are reading this book. But stop for a moment to consider the amount of time you may be spending each month searching for various documents as you need them. What should take a few seconds may take hours. Perhaps you finally find that mortgage document . . . in the car-payment file. Or maybe you give up after not finding it at all.

Frustrating, isn't it? Now imagine that it's sometime in the future and you are no longer on the scene. Your spouse, adult child, or another loved one is urgently trying to locate a key financial record or a document with your final instructions or your will or trust documents. Imagine the unnecessary time, anxiety, uncertainty, and expense that person is experiencing at what is likely the most devastating time of his or her life . . . because of the financial clutter you may have left behind.

Make the Impossible a Little Easier

John was a robust man in his late thirties, a good husband and father, and a conscientious provider. He always paid his bills on time and made sure his family's needs were met. But then the unthinkable happened. One cold, icy evening on the way home from work, John's car hit a patch of black ice and spun out of control. He died instantly when the car crashed head-on into a pickup truck in the opposite lane.

In the surreal haze of shock and disbelief that accompanies sudden loss, John's wife, Karen, began the painful process of settling his financial affairs. She quickly realized that, despite their best intentions, she and John had never taken the time to organize their personal and financial papers for easy accessibility. While John had a will, Karen was not sure where it was located or, since it had not been reviewed in several years, whether it reflected John's most recent wishes. As a result, Karen experienced an additional burden that no grieving survivor should have to bear: the exhausting anxiety and frustration of searching for documents and instructions she needed in order to ensure that her own financial life could go on.

This is the key reason why reducing financial clutter and keeping your financial house in order are so important: If your records are scattered between drawer and closet and basement and crawlspace, can you imagine how tough it will be for your spouse or other family members to sort through your affairs if something happens to you? As you seek to avoid the common Stupid Mistakes of personal finance, let me suggest that one of the most responsible, loving things you can do for your family is to make sure that all of your key records and documents are organized, accessible, and up to date.

In case you don't enjoy thinking about your own demise, there's another compelling reason for getting your records in order: the simple fact that you need to refer to them often during your lifetime. The fact is, you may be around for decades to come. So why not make life a little easier for yourself as well as for your loved ones? Get those records in order, and you'll be able to find documents in seconds instead of standing on your head as you search the bottoms of boxes in your basement. And as new paperwork flows into your life, as it does with nearly every day's mail, you'll be able to file it within seconds instead of tossing it in that precipitous pile of "things you'll take care of Someday."

Eliminating financial clutter and preparing to leave your house in order involve:

- turning your financial pile into a financial file;

- writing or updating your will;

- establishing a durable power of attorney, health-care proxy, and living will; and, in many cases,

- setting up a living trust.

Don't be intimidated. I'll help you set up your home financial file; then we'll consider what you need to know about the other components of estate planning.

Your Home Financial File

Your first step is to hop into the family buggy and drive to Wal-Mart. Say "howdy" to the friendly greeter, go to the office-supplies aisle, and pick up a dozen or so blank file folders and file labels. Then proceed to the candy aisle and select a bag of your favorite M&M's. (See, getting organized can be fun after all.)

The next stop is your neighborhood bank where, if you don't already have one, you're going to rent a safe-deposit box. It will run you $20 to $65 per year, depending on how big a box you want, but a safe-deposit box is a good investment. (Almost as good as the M&M's.)

When you return home with folders, labels, and safe-deposit key in hand (I'm assuming that, if you're like me, the M&M's are now long gone), grab a pen and label each file folder. If you tend to write in tongues, you may want to type the labels to make your folders legible. Here's how you'll label each file tab:

1. *Personal Information and Instructions*
2. *Personal Documents (copies)*
3. *Personal Insurance Policies*
4. *Property Insurance Policies*
5. *Household Inventory and Net Worth*
6. *Savings and Investment Records*
7. *Retirement Programs*
8. *Consumer-Debt Records*
9. *Car Ownership and Repair Records*
10. *Real Estate Purchases and Improvements*
11. *Tax Returns and Documentation*
12. *Wills and Trusts (copies)*

It's likely that you do not yet have everything listed above. For example, you may not yet own a home or other real estate. But you probably will someday, and if you maintain the file as suggested, the folder will be waiting for you when the time comes.

You'll note that in several instances I recommend keeping *copies* of certain documents in your home financial file. That's because the original documents are extremely valuable, and, unless you have your own fireproof safe at home, you'll want to keep certain originals in your safe-deposit box or with your attorney to protect them from loss, fire, or theft. It may mean two or three trips to a photocopier during the next few days, but they will be minutes and dimes well spent.

Now it's time to root through your file drawers, under your mattress, in the trunk of your car, and wherever else you've been tossing financial records to begin gathering documents for the folders you've labeled.

Folder #1: Personal Information and Instructions

In the event of your death, this folder is likely the first one your surviving loved ones will see. It will provide two key items to get them started: (1) an up-to-date list of important personal information and (2) instructions from you.

Personal Information. Take out a couple of sheets of paper and invest a half-hour preparing a list detailing:

- your full legal name;
- your date and place of birth;
- your Social Security number;
- your military service number and dates of service;
- your date and place of marriage;
- the names, birth dates, addresses, and phone numbers of your children; and
- the names, addresses, and phone numbers of your former spouses and the children of previous marriages.

You'll also want to list essential medical information such as the names and phone numbers of your doctors and what each physician treats you for. Also list the names, addresses, and phone numbers of your key advisers such as your attorney, accountant, financial planner, minister, insurance agents, and executor.

If you have given someone power of attorney (which authorizes that person to control your assets if you become incapacitated) or named a health-care proxy (someone you've authorized to make health-care decisions on your behalf), name those people here and list their phone numbers and addresses.

Provide phone numbers for the Social Security Administration (800-772-1213) and, if you served in the military, the Veterans Administration (800-827-1000). These numbers will help your survivors process requests for Social Security and veterans death benefits.

Write down the location of the original of your most recent will (most likely your attorney's office) as well as the location of a copy (folder #12 in your home financial file).

Finally, write down the location of your safe-deposit box and keys.

Instructions. Your letter of instruction should be kept with your will, but a copy should be kept in this file as well. (Quite often, wills are not referred to until several days *after* a memorial service and burial.) Your attorney can assist you in drafting this letter, but it is not necessary for you to use an attorney. Here you will detail your final wishes and any prior arrangements you may have made regarding funeral or memorial services and burial or cremation. You can also include a special message of love and encouragement for family members, notes regarding whom to call to begin processing insurance claims, and even a note bequeathing your Guinness-record toothpick collection to your cousin Jimmy if your will has not already done so.

Folder #2: Personal Documents

Photocopies of your birth certificate, marriage certificate, and divorce papers (all essential in estate settlement), adoption papers, and military discharge papers should be stored here. Keep the originals in your safe-deposit box. In the spirit of government efficiency, we all need our birth certificates to prove we were born. If you do not have your birth certificate, check with your parents. If they can't prove you were born, check with the hospital and/or city government where you think you may have been born.

Folder #3: Personal Insurance Policies

Policies and payment records on life, health/medical, disability, and other personal ("people") insurance policies go in this folder, along with employer-provided policy and benefits booklets.

Since your insurance coverage and/or policies could change frequently due to job changes or prudent rate shopping, be sure to keep this folder up-to-date, clearly indicating which policies are in force and which have expired or been canceled. Mark the expiration date clearly on the front of expired or canceled policies and keep them for a few years in case of a delayed claim; then discard them.

Keep payment records (premium-payment receipts with their canceled checks) in this file as well, attaching records to the appropriate policy. This will verify that policies were paid and kept in force.

Folder #4: Property Insurance Policies

This folder is for policies and payment records on your homeowners or renters insurance, auto insurance, umbrella liability insurance, and insurance on other properties. As with all insurance, keep these policies updated as your circumstances change. Follow the advice above regarding payment records and canceled or expired policies.

Folder #5: Household Inventory and Net Worth

Whether you're renting or buying your home, you should always maintain an up-to-date inventory of major furnishings, appliances, jewelry, artwork—anything that would be costly or difficult to replace in the event of theft or fire. A copy of that inventory will go in this file; keep the original in your safe-deposit box.

A household inventory can take some time to complete, but doing it conscientiously can pay huge dividends in the long term. Plus, you have to do it only once; then you simply update your inventory as you acquire new items or dispose of old ones. The easiest way is to go from room to room, including your basement and garage, listing your major possessions complete with their brand names, serial numbers, purchase dates, and purchase prices. If you do not have receipts, or warranty registrations verifying prices and dates, look for canceled checks or credit card statements that provide this information. If you're normal, you'll have several items for which no records have been kept; estimate their prices and purchase dates as accurately as you can.

Many people back up their inventories with photos or home videos of each item. Photographs can be especially helpful to police or insurance adjusters should you need their help. Keep photos or videocassettes in your safe-deposit box along with the original inventory list.

Also in this folder, keep a copy of your current net worth statement.

Update your household inventory every time you acquire a major new possession or get rid of an old one. You'll also want to update your net worth statement at least once a year.

Folder #6: Savings and Investment Records

This folder is for documents and statements regarding your savings programs and for any investments *other than* real estate or retirement plans—stocks, bonds, mutual funds, precious metals, rare coins, and so on. You'll want to keep actual securities documents, as well as any precious metals, in your safe-deposit box; buy/sell records on stocks, bonds, mutual funds, rare coins, precious metals, or other investments can go in your home file.

Buy/sell records should include the date of purchase, quantity, item, purchase price and commission paid, selling price and commission paid, and profit or loss. These records are essential at income-tax time and in the thrilling event of an IRS audit.

Folder #7: Retirement Programs

Documents and statements from 401(k)s, 403(b)s, pension programs, Individual Retirement Accounts, SEP-IRAs, and Keogh plans go here.

Folder #8: Consumer-Debt Records

Keep account numbers, statements, and payment records for your consumer debts in this folder. (This will include credit cards, charge cards, and financing on anything—other than cars—that does not appreciate in value.) Also keep copies of correspondence you've sent and received regarding your accounts—especially letters in which (1) you've asked to have your account closed and (2) the credit issuer has confirmed that your account has been closed *at your request*. By ridding your life of Stupid Mistake #5, "Borrowing Trouble," you're going to render this entire file inactive as soon as possible.

Folder #9: Car Ownership and Repair Records

Folder #9 is for pink slips, registration receipts, purchase agreements, warranties, and other ownership documents for all your vehicles. It's also wise to keep copies of all service and repair records in case the repair work done three weeks ago needs to be redone.

Folder #10: Real Estate Purchases and Improvements

When you went to the closing on your house, you were handed a forest of paper and told to "just sign here." You took home a thick folder of documents along with a fresh case of carpal tunnel syndrome; you'll want to keep photocopies of all those documents in this file. This is also where you'll keep copies of deeds and improvement records on any rental properties, raw land, or other real-estate investments. Original deeds should be kept in your safe-deposit box.

You May Be Making
Stupid Mistake #11 If . . .

- your loved ones would not know where to find your key accounts, records, and documents if you should become seriously injured by killed

- you frequently find yourself crawling among the dust bunnies under your bed in search of important legal and financial records

- you have not completed a home inventory or updated it within the past two years

- you do not have a written will or have not had your will reviewed and updated recently by an estate-planning attorney

- you have not designated a durable power of attorney and health-care proxy

---

Also in this folder, start a list of improvements you make to your property. Record the date, type, and cost of all improvements and attach receipts verifying this information. This will come in handy whenever your house is appraised for sale or refinancing, and in some cases it may be needed when you file tax returns after selling the house.

Folder #11: Tax Returns and Documentation

A normal IRS audit (oxymoron) can dig into your past up to three years if your friendly tax person suspects a "good faith" error. However, he has six years to challenge your return if he thinks you underreported your income by 25 percent or more. If fraud is suspected, he can hound you as far back as your previous life and as far into the future as your next one. Moral: Keep your tax records indefinitely.

Keep the last two years' returns and documentation (W-2 forms, 1099s, receipts, expense records) in this folder for easy access throughout the year. In a storage box in your closet or basement, keep *a minimum* of four more years' tax records. Better yet, keep 'em forever.

If you should lose these returns, your tax-return preparer or the IRS and state tax agencies can provide you with copies. However, they have copies only of the actual tax forms you filled out and not the receipts you totaled to claim your deductions. So keep the originals of receipts in a safe place, clearly labeled so they are easy to find for a given claim in a given year.

Folder #12: Wills and Trusts

Keep photocopies here, along with the name, address, and phone number of the attorney who drew up the documents. Originals should be kept with your attorney, who most likely has a stationary, fireproof safe. It's generally not wise to keep originals of wills and trusts in your safe-deposit box because, in some situations, banks can seal safe-deposit boxes until other estate matters have been addressed. Store originals of wills and trusts at home *only* if you have a stationary, fireproof safe. Keep in mind that laws change and your personal situation and wishes change; therefore, wills and trusts should be reviewed every few years by your attorney to ensure they are up-to-date.

Customize, Adapt to Your Needs

Of course, I want you to feel free to customize and adapt your home financial file as your situation changes. As the file grows, you may want to further classify your records by using twelve hanging files with multiple folders in each hanging file.

Keep your home financial file in a file cabinet that's near where you process mail and pay bills. Whenever you need the information, it'll be right there. More importantly, your home financial file will be readily accessible should something happen to you, making a difficult task much easier for your loved ones.

Now there are some additional steps to consider in the process of eliminating financial clutter from your life—some key planning tools that can help organize and protect your financial assets not only for today, but also for the benefit of your loved ones in the event of your incapacitation or death.

Why You Need a Will

It's true that you can't take it with you when you die, which underscores the point that money is only a tool of life, not life itself, and that relationships with God, family, and friends deserve our highest priority. Once you've breathed your last, there are basically three places your financial assets can go: (1) to your heirs, (2) to a ministry or charity, or (3) to the government. Who gets what, and how much, will be determined largely by whether you have drafted a will spelling out how you want your assets divided.

Whether you realize it or not, you do have a will. If you've been proactive, you've drafted and signed a will detailing your final wishes for your property. If you have not drafted and signed a will, then your state will, in effect, "write" one for you after you die, using what it calls "intestate succession rules." (Dying intestate simply means you've croaked without a will.) Typically, states give assets to the surviving spouse and children (in most cases a fifty-fifty split); if there is no surviving spouse or children, then dibs go to grandchildren, parents, siblings, nieces and nephews, and cousins, in that order. If there are no surviving relatives, your assets go to the state.

So why be proactive and draft a will? Because you care about your loved ones and your property, and you don't want your state to determine who gets what. (Neither do you want to put your loved ones through the lengthy, expensive process in which the state divides and distributes your assets.) Most likely you have better ideas about where you want your money and property to go—especially if you're a surviving spouse and you prefer to designate beneficiaries other than your children or relatives. Perhaps you'd prefer that your favorite charity receive a good portion of your estate instead of your cheesy cousin Louie.

When you draft your will, you'll need to designate an executor who will serve as your personal representative and ensure that the will is probated (put through the legal system) and that your estate is distributed according to the terms of the will. You'll want to select someone you trust, who has an eye for detail, and who has your survivors' best interests at heart. The executor can and should be paid a fair fee from your estate for his or her time and effort on your behalf.

Depending on the complexity of your situation, a will can cost between

$100 and $3,000 if done by a lawyer. The law does not require you to use an attorney, but most financial advisers strongly recommend that you do to be sure the essential bases are covered. You can also draft a will using one of several software programs or a form kit from a stationery store. In any case, you will need to have two witnesses (in some states, three) watch you sign the will and sign their own names attesting to that fact. If you do draft your will yourself, I strongly recommend that you hire an attorney to review it to be sure there are no loopholes that could cause trouble for your survivors.

A Durable Power of Attorney

It's a situation none of us likes to think about: becoming incapacitated by an accident, illness, or old age and rendered incapable of handling our personal and financial affairs.

If this should happen to you, a court order may appoint a guardian to manage your affairs for you. Problem: The court-appointed guardian could be Lenny, your freeloader son who's lived in your basement since dropping out of high school fifteen years ago and who would give his favorite nose ring to get his hands on your checkbook.

You can keep Lenny away from your assets by appointing your own guardian through a durable power of attorney. This document authorizes someone you trust to step in and handle your personal and financial affairs on your behalf should you become unable to carry out these responsibilities yourself. It's another proactive step we can all take to help ensure good stewardship of our assets and to help reduce the stress on our loved ones.

You can also set up special powers of attorney, designating different people to handle different responsibilities. You could appoint one guardian to make decisions on your behalf regarding health care, another to handle housing and personal property situations, and another to manage your finances.

You can change or cancel a durable power of attorney at any time. Since it is set up to protect your assets while you're alive but incapacitated, it terminates immediately after you die.

A Living Trust

An alternative to a durable power of attorney is a living trust, which effectively accomplishes the same objective as a power of attorney but with a significant, additional benefit: It remains effective after you die and passes your assets directly to your beneficiaries without the time, hassle, and expense of probate.

A trust is a legal entity into which you can place the title to your property and nonretirement plan assets, yet you have full use and stewardship of those assets throughout your life. In most cases financial advisers recommend the revocable living trust, which allows you to change or cancel its provisions at any time. You can add new assets or pull assets out. If you become incapacitated, the trust is managed for you by a successor trustee of your choosing, much like the guardian in a durable power of attorney. In the event of your death, the trust and its assets go directly to your beneficiaries, steering clear of costly probate.

If you set up a revocable living trust, you will still need a will—although of a slightly different flavor. The pour-over (or backup) will addresses any assets that may have been left out of the revocable living trust (either by mistake or by passage of time as new assets are accumulated).

A Living Will

Another living nightmare we don't like to contemplate is that of becoming terminal through illness or accident but being kept alive indefinitely by life-prolonging medical machinery. Setting up a living will can help guide medical personnel as well as your loved ones in the tough decisions they would face in such a situation.

Also known as a health-care power of attorney or an advance directive, a living will informs your doctors and family that if recovery appears impossible you do not want extraordinary life-extending procedures to be implemented. It is a document signed by yourself and by witnesses, and it also appoints a friend or loved one whom you trust to make sure your wishes are carried out.

Don't Try This at Home

Although wills, powers of attorney, and living wills can be set up using forms or software, I strongly recommend that you consult an attorney on all such matters. Do-it-yourself documents are sometimes the first to be thrown out of court, and with them can go all your good intentions and best wishes. Because estate planning is complex (let alone dull), a good attorney is well worth his or her fee in helping you determine the combination and design of wills, powers of attorney, and/or trusts that will prove best for your situation and needs.

Peace of Mind

Getting your home financial file, wills and trusts, powers of attorney, and health-care directives together and up-to-date will take some effort, but your investment of time and money will be well worth the newfound sense of order that comes to your financial life. Key documents will be readily available whenever you or your loved ones need them. Your family and your assets will be better protected from unthinkables such as premature death or incapacitation. Most importantly, you and your family will enjoy peace of mind in knowing that, because you love them, you've made provisions now that will help provide for the legal and financial contingencies in their future.

Playing "Someday" with Your Retirement

*Teach us to number our days and
recognize how few they are; help us
to spend them as we should.*

—PSALM 90:12 TLB

Ah, retirement. Serene visions of saying good-bye to the boss and the coworkers and the career stress. Of rising at the crack of 9:30, lounging with the paper over coffee, then driving to the golf course to chase the small white ball. Of sitting on the patio and not having to go anywhere if you don't want to. Of more time watching, reading to, and playing with the grandchildren. Of napping when you feel like it, waking in time for the Early Bird Special, and staying up as late as you want or going to bed as early as you want. Of taking that cruise you've always wanted to take or touring the art galleries of Europe or driving cross-country in an RV. Of volunteering your time and talent for a mission or charity that's close to your heart.

Almost all of us will retire from our full-time jobs. It could be that the workplace dictates our departure, or possibly our own inner clocks tell us. It may happen early, it may happen in our midsixties, or it may be "late." Regardless, the day is likely to come when the steady paycheck is suddenly replaced by a twenty-minute party with cake and a silly "So You're Retiring" card signed by all.

As I mentioned earlier, it's a high probability that your retirement years will be the biggest expense of your life. More expensive than the biggest house you ever buy, and maybe even more expensive than a coffee at Starbucks. Thanks to modern medicine and preventive care, we're living longer. As today's working population draws closer to retirement time, it is likely that most of us will spend at least twenty years in retirement mode. For many, it could be thirty years or even longer. Almost *one-third* of our lives.

And all without another paycheck.

Will you be financially ready for this major life change? Will you be in a position to support the retirement lifestyle you want to lead for twenty or thirty years?

According to the U.S. Census Bureau, almost half of all Americans over age sixty-five have a household income below $15,000 a year. Only 18 percent have annual incomes of more than $35,000. These figures include Social Security benefits. In what should be some of the most fulfilling years of their lives, too many retirees struggle to make ends meet, monitoring their mailboxes for every Social Security check while hoping and praying that they will not outlive their money.

Today's workers, however, are blessed with incentive-heavy retirement savings plans that older generations did not have. IRAs, 401(k)s, and other programs provide generous tax incentives to encourage us to save and invest for a financially secure future. However, a recent report from SunAmerica made some startling revelations:

- Fourteen percent of baby boomers aged forty-seven to fifty-five and 20 percent of those aged thirty-seven to forty-six have saved nothing for retirement.

- Among Americans of all ages, approximately 40 percent haven't even tried to calculate what they might need in order to live comfortably in their retirement years.

- Of those who have company-sponsored retirement savings plans, fewer than 50 percent participate in those plans.

Chances are, we'll receive some form of Social Security income once we retire. But we've already seen that Social Security will be only a small stipend—*a minimal safety net* that won't come close to covering our cost of living when the paychecks stop. Neither should we count on defined-benefit pensions or inheritances to make up the shortfall in our later years. Hoping that someone else will finance our retirement, or that a ship of some kind will sail in to rescue us, is simply the Stupid Mistake of counting on the illusive "someday."

Whether we thrive or strive financially during retirement is mostly up to us. The level of financial freedom we enjoy in our retirement years depends on what we do *today*—and for the rest of our working lives—in preparation for tomorrow.

Questions to Ponder—But Not for Too Long

In the past, retirement planners have suggested that our monthly expenses in retirement are likely to fall between 70 and 90 percent of our preretirement expenses. This scenario counted on some of our work-related expenses going away, such as the costs of an office wardrobe, commuting, child care, and daily lunches. Lately, however, planners have recognized that retirement living expenses could actually be 100 to 120 percent or higher, especially in the earlier years when retirees may want to travel more or take on other long-postponed adventures.

To help you begin to get specific about your projected income needs, let me suggest five key questions to consider.

1. *At what age would you like to retire?* Don't think in terms of age sixty-five simply because this has been the traditional retirement age since 1935. In fact, people are working longer, and surveys have indicated that the majority of baby boomers intend to continue working at least part time after they've officially retired from their full-time professions. The longer you work, the more you can contribute to your retirement nest egg . . . and the fewer years you'll have to self-finance.

2. *When that blessed day arrives, what major obligations will you have?* Will your house be paid for, or will you need to continue making mortgage or rent payments? Will your kids be out of the nest and out of college? Have you drawn a clear line, or do you plan to continue supporting them through endless schooling, false starts in the job market, or single

parenthood? Will you be caring for aging parents? Make your best prediction based on your circumstances; any of these factors will increase your income needs.

3. *What kind of lifestyle do you want in retirement?* Do you want to stay put or move to another part of the country? Do you want a quiet life, staying mostly around house and yard, or do you want to hit the road, visiting places you've always wanted to see? How about returning to school? Are you hoping to volunteer at the church or in your community? Your retirement lifestyle will go a long way toward determining the annual income you'll need.

4. *Will you continue working?* Many retirees find that after the initial euphoria of leaving the work force, they become bored and restless. The sudden absence of a daily sense of mission could easily make you feel as though you've been put out to pasture. Continuing to work in some capacity, at least seasonally or part time, can help stretch your financial reserves in retirement. It's also bound to keep you sharper and healthier as you learn new skills and continue to interact with people.

5. *How long will you live?* Dumb question, but an important consideration. If you're in good health and your parents and grandparents were active into their late eighties or nineties, it's possible you could live three decades or more in retirement mode. I suggest being conservative and optimistic here: Plan to live to age ninety-five or one hundred so you don't draw down your retirement savings too quickly.

How Much Annual Income Will You Need?

Retirement-income projections are likely to change significantly as the time draws nearer, but the following projection can provide you with a starting point for determining (1) the annual income you may need when retirement time begins and (2) the amount you will need to have saved by then to provide that annual income. Grab a calculator and take these simple steps with me:

1. Add up all your present monthly expenses.

$_____

2. Subtract major expenses you probably won't face once you've entered retirement: contributions to retirement plans, children's college costs, mortgage payments (if you're on course to pay off your house), credit card debt payments, etc.

Result: $_____

3. Multiply the result by 12.

$_____

4. Now add up all your quarterly, semiannual, and annual expenses such as insurance premiums, association fees, property taxes, and Christmas:

$_____

5. Add 3 and 4 to arrive at your

Total Current Annual Expenses: $_____

6. Multiply your total current annual expenses by

- 75 to 80 percent if your mortgage will be paid in full, all other debt will be paid in full, and you foresee a relatively modest, home-based lifestyle.

- 80 to 100 percent if your mortgage will be mostly paid off, all other debt will be paid off, and you foresee continuing your present lifestyle.

- 100 to 120 percent if you'll be taking on a new mortgage of any size, you don't think you'll have other debt fully paid off, or you foresee an adventurous, higher-expense lifestyle.

Percentage selected: ___%
Total Projected Annual Expenses: $_____

7. Tax time. Multiply your total projected annual expenses by your present federal marginal tax bracket of_____ percent.

Projected Annual Federal Tax: $_____

8. Estimate your *state tax* in the same way.

Projected State Tax: $_____

9. Now add your projected annual federal and state taxes to your total projected annual expenses.

Annual Retirement Income Needed: $_____

How Big a Nest Egg Will You Need?

Now you have a ballpark idea, in today's dollars, of the annual income you may need in order to support yourself in retirement. Social Security will probably supply a small portion of this income. If you were to retire today at full eligibility, you would receive approximately $12,000 per year per working spouse (a spouse without sufficient Social Security "credits" will receive about $6,000). Keep in mind that these figures are in today's dollars; they are subject to indexing for inflation and could also change as Congress tinkers with the system.

But to play it conservatively, we won't factor Social Security income into our projections here. We'll pretend that by the time you retire, either the system will have gone down the tubes or Congress, in its wisdom, will have raised the age of eligibility to ninety-eight and a half.

Now you'll want to fasten your seat belt. It's time to determine the kind of lump sum you'll need to build between now and retirement day—a sum that can consistently spin off enough investment income to meet your projected annual income needs. (I should warn you that the projected lump sum will seem huge, perhaps even unattainable. That's why we're talking *today*, not Someday. But you may be encouraged if you go back to the tables at the end of Chapter 7 and play with the variables to see the potential of your four powerful friends at work.)

To estimate your Big Sum, let's assume that during the first ten or fifteen years of retirement you will try to keep your principal intact and rely only on investment earnings for your income. And let's assume that during these initial years you will be able to earn at least 6 percent average annual return on your invested principal. Here's the equation:

$ Annual Retirement Income Needed divided by .06 [6 percent]

=

$ Total "Big Sum" Needed on Retirement Day

John and Teresa, for example, project they will need an annual retirement income of $55,000. They enter $55,000 into their calculator. Then, assuming a 6 percent average annual return on investment during the first ten to fifteen years of retirement, they divide $55,000 by .06. The resulting figure is $916,667. Sounds like a ton of money, and it is. But if John and Teresa harness the powers of priority, tax-advantaged saving, equity investing, and compounding over time, they have a good chance of attaining that goal. If they then average 6 percent and don't invade their principal, their retirement funds could spin off $55,000 per year indefinitely, leaving the $916,667 essentially intact until later in life.

The projections we're making are in today's dollars and are meant to provide only quick, general "snapshots." I've provided them simply to get you thinking about the challenge, and the potential, of preparing for retirement. For more precise help in projecting income needs and savings goals, let me suggest you use one of the excellent retirement planning calculators available on several Web sites including www.quicken.com, www.smartmoney.com, www.fidelity.com, and www.vanguard.com. Any projections should be reviewed and adjusted annually to account for inflation or changing circumstances.

Are You Saving Enough?

You may recall that in Chapter 7 the following general targets were suggested for saving for retirement:

Percent of Gross Income to Save for Retirement

up to age 35	at least 5 percent
age 35 to 45	at least 10 percent
age 45 to 55	at least 15 percent
age 55+	at least 20 percent

You May Be Making
Stupid Mistake #12 If . . .

○ you've tended to think that life's too costly now and retirement will have to take care of itself

○ you believe Social Security will meet your needs as you grow older

○ you've never calculated how much you'll need for your retirement years

○ you're thirty-five or older and are not regularly contributing to a tax-advantaged retirement savings plan

○ you're forty-five or older and are not making the maximum annual contributions to your 401(k), 403(b), 457, and/or Individual Retirement Accounts

○ you have few plans for how you want to spend your days in retirement

---

Are you saving enough today for your retirement tomorrow? Do you need to shift some financial priorities—perhaps stop feeding the monster—in order to save more diligently? You can't start too early, and the more you can put to work today, the less you'll have to hustle as you approach retirement time. And if you're thirty-five or older, it's *definitely* time to get serious about growing your Big Sum for retirement.

Fortunately, this is where your four powerful friends really step up to help make your efforts worthwhile.

Saving for Retirement

What would you think if I told you of a savings vehicle in which you could receive an immediate 15 to 28 percent cash return on your money—*and* the distinct possibility of earning an average of 8 to 12 percent or more annually?

No, it's not some exotic offshore tax haven. The savings vehicles that offer these possibilities come to you courtesy of that feisty uncle of ours, Uncle Sam, through tax-advantaged savings programs such as the 401(k), 403(b), and IRAs.

One day, Uncle Sam wasn't feeling quite like himself, and an amazing thing happened. He established a set of programs to actually encourage individuals and families to save part of their earnings for the retirement years. Bless his heart, and all his other vital organs, for he even provided incentives by making some contributions *tax-deductible* and all earnings *tax-deferred*, which can carve hundreds of dollars off each year's tax bill and help our savings compound much more dramatically.

In addition, virtually every plan can be set up so that your contributions are *automatically* made for you, before you even see, hold, or spend the money. If the plan is sponsored by your employer, he will deduct your designated contribution from your gross salary each payday and send it to your savings plan; this amount is not taxed as part of your income. So as you pay yourself first, automatically, you're also paying less in taxes.

For John and Teresa, there are multiple benefits to these tax-advantaged savings plans. John has a 401(k) plan at his place of employment. This year he'll contribute a total of $6,000 to the plan, or 12 percent of his $50,000 gross salary. (He hopes to increase his contribution to 15 percent next year.) John has authorized his employer to direct $230.77 to the plan from each of his twenty-six paychecks (the power of priority).

John and Teresa's combined income puts them in the 28 percent tax bracket. But John's $6,000 total annual contribution is *tax-deductible*, so he does not owe income tax on that amount. This virtually gives him an immediate return on investment of 28 percent, or $1,680 (the power of tax-advantaged saving).

The benefits don't stop with the immediate return of 28 percent. John has directed his 401(k) provider to place his money in a couple of mutual funds that have the potential of earning an annualized compounded return of between 8 and 12 percent. Because these earnings are all *tax deferred* until John and Teresa begin withdrawing the money in their retirement, he'll be able to keep more money compounding over time — interest on principal, interest on interest (the powers of tax-advantaged saving, equity investing, and compounding).

The tables at the end of Chapter 7 demonstrate the positive snowball effect of disciplined, tax-advantaged saving through plans such as John's 401(k). And there's an array of retirement savings vehicles to choose from.

Company Savings Plans

The 401(k). We owe a debt of gratitude to a bright young consultant named Ted Benna, who developed the idea for the 401(k) after studying section 401(k) of that scintillating fireside read, the United States Tax Code. Uncle Sam gave the program its approval in 1986, revolutionizing the retirement savings game for tens of millions of ordinary people.

401(k)s are for employees of for-profit companies. Your employer provides a form on which you authorize him to deduct up to 15 percent of your gross salary from each paycheck. This percentage can total up to $11,000 in 2002; the annual limit is scheduled to increase to $12,000 in 2003, $13,000 in 2004, $14,000 in 2005, and $15,000 in 2006. Subsequent annual increases will be indexed for inflation in increments of $500. (Since this is Congress we're talking about, these amounts are subject to change. Always confirm each year's limit with your plan administrator.)

Per your instructions on the sign-up form, each contribution is invested in one or more mutual funds offered by the plan. But it gets even better. Many employers, although not required to do so, offer programs in which they match your contribution to your 401(k) up to 5 to 6 percent of your gross salary. In John's case, his employer matches his contribution 100 percent up to 5 percent of his gross salary, which will add another $2,500 to John's plan this year.

Some employers allow new employees to begin 401(k) contributions immediately or within their first ninety days; others require a one-year waiting period. Obviously, you'll want to begin funding your 401(k) the moment you're eligible to do so and contribute the maximum as quickly as your cash flow allows.

The 403(b). Also named after a section of the tax code, the 403(b) is designed for employees of nonprofit organizations. This plan allows contributions of up to 20 percent of gross salary, with the same annual dollar limits as the 401(k). Contributions are tax-deductible, earnings are tax-deferred, and you'll enjoy most of the other benefits and investment opportunities afforded by a 401(k). If you work for a nonprofit organization, take full advantage of your 403(b) savings opportunity as soon as you qualify.

The 457. No, this isn't an airplane. It's a 401(k)-type retirement savings plan for government employees. Same contribution limits, same tax benefits.

Individual Retirement Accounts

While Individual Retirement Accounts (IRAs) have been around awhile, they now come in a variety of flavors.

The Traditional IRA. Any wage earner, regardless of whether he has a company-sponsored retirement plan, can open and contribute to a traditional IRA each year. You can contribute up to $3,000 each year until 2005, when the limit increases to $4,000. It's scheduled to increase again in 2008, to $5,000, after which contribution limits will be indexed for inflation. Contributions to a traditional IRA are fully tax-deductible *if you do not have a retirement plan at work.* If you do have a company-sponsored retirement plan, you can still contribute on a tax-deductible or partially deductible basis if your adjusted gross income (AGI) doesn't exceed a specified limit. These AGI limits will increase each year until 2005, when they'll hold at $65,000 for couples and $50,000 for singles. Anyone can contribute to a *nondeductible* traditional IRA, regardless of his or her income.

Because 401(k)s and 403(b)s allow tax deductibility and may also offer employer matching, you'll first want to maximize contributions to any company plans before you contribute anything to a nondeductible IRA. But any funds you do put in IRAs will still enjoy the benefits of priority, tax deferral, equity investing, and compounding.

IRAs can be set up through banks, insurance companies, brokerage firms, and mutual fund families. You can even sign up for a monthly draft from your checking account to give yourself the "pay yourself first" advantage.

The Spousal IRA. This IRA for the "nonworking spouse" also allows contributions up to $3,000 per year. If one spouse has not earned income *or* is not covered by a company plan, couples with adjusted gross incomes up to $150,000 may contribute to a spousal IRA on a fully tax-deductible basis. As with other IRAs, taxes are deferred on earnings.

The Roth IRA. The new Roth IRA allows couples with adjusted gross incomes up to $150,000 and singles with AGIs up to $90,000 to contribute the same annual amounts as a traditional IRA, regardless of whether they're covered by company retirement plans. The big exception with the Roth is that your contributions are *not tax-deductible*. The trade-off is that you receive a major benefit when you're withdrawing the funds during retirement: Instead of simply deferring taxes on your investment earnings, the Roth IRA eliminates them completely. Your earnings in a Roth are income tax–free. What you miss on the front end, you more than make up on the back end.

The SEP-IRA. With the dramatic increase in self-employment and small businesses on the side, the SEP-IRA is worth serious consideration for anyone who earns self-employment income.

The Simplified Employee Pension is designed for small businesses or people who have self-employment income. With a SEP-IRA you can contribute up to 13.04 percent of self-employment income, after deductions, with annual dollar limits subject to change. If you have employees, you must contribute the same percentage of their pay to their accounts as the percentage of your pay you're contributing for yourself. Contributions are tax-deductible, investment choices are similar to those of 401(k)s and IRAs, and earnings are tax-deferred until withdrawal.

The Keogh. Another, older plan for the self-employed is the Keogh. Depending on the Keogh program you set up (there are variations to choose from), a Keogh allows you to contribute up to 20 percent of self-employment income to a limit of $30,000 per year. More paperwork is required in setting up and administering a Keogh, but it may be worth your while, especially if your potential contribution surpasses the contribution limit of a SEP-IRA.

The Geezer Special

For those who are fifty or older, there are some special "catch-up" provisions that allow you to contribute even more to several of the above plans. If you turned fifty before or during 2002, you can put an additional $500 in your IRA each year. In 2006, the catch-up provision allows $1,000.

You can also put an additional $1,000 in your 401(k), 403(b), or 457 plan in 2002. (There are some restrictions on 403(b)s). Those catch-up contributions are scheduled to increase by $1,000 each year through 2006, after which they will be indexed for inflation in increments of $500.

You're Probably Eligible for Multiple Plans

Depending on your circumstances, you may be able to combine two or more plans in order to increase your total annual contributions.

For example, in John's 401(k) program, his company matches his contributions up to 5 percent of his annual salary. Teresa teaches in the public school system and thus is eligible for a 403(b) plan. John and Teresa can:

(1) contribute up to 15 percent of John's gross annual salary to his 401(k) and receive matching benefits *and*

(2) contribute up to 20 percent of Teresa's gross annual salary to her 403(b) *and*

(3) each contribute up to the annual limit in either traditional IRAs or Roth IRAs. (Contributions to IRAs would be *nondeductible* in their case because John and Teresa participate in company plans, but they can still reap the other long-term benefits. In John and Teresa's case, the Roth would be preferable because all its earnings are completely tax-free.)

Let's look at Dick and Jennifer's situation. Dick has a 401(k) at work; Jennifer is a stay-at-home mom who home-schools her young children. Dick and Jennifer can:

(1) contribute up to 15 percent of Dick's gross annual salary to his 401(k) and receive employer matching *and*

(2) contribute the annual limit, tax-deductible, to a spousal IRA for Jennifer *and*

(3) contribute the annual limit for Dick, non-tax-deductible, to either a traditional IRA or a Roth IRA. (In Dick's case, a Roth would again be preferable to a traditional IRA because with Roths all earnings are completely tax-free.)

If John, Teresa, Dick, or Jennifer is fifty or older, he or she can also take advantage of the catch-up provisions, detailed above, to put more money to work for retirement.

There's a variety of possible combinations, and it would be prudent to have a retirement planning professional look over your personal situation and advise you of your options. The fundamental rule, however, is to take full advantage of available tax deductibility and employer matching in 401(k), 403(b), or 457 plans *before* contributing to any of the Individual Retirement Accounts.

Borrow from Retirement Savings? Don't Do It.

With very few exceptions, if you withdraw funds from a 401(k)-type plan before the age of fifty-nine and a half, you'll be docked a penalty of 10 percent of the amount withdrawn *and* pay the income tax on that amount.

And the exceptions aren't really worthy of serious consideration. 401(k)-type plans allow you to take out (and pay back) a loan from your account. While this is lauded as a benefit, it's really not a good idea. A loan sets back your savings and compounding momentum; in addition, if you leave or are terminated by your employer, he can effectively "call" the loan, requiring full payback of the outstanding balance within sixty days of your departure. If you don't meet this payback schedule, both the IRS and your company will get nasty. It's just not worth it. Keep your 401(k) intact and growing and, if a loan becomes absolutely necessary in the future, borrow elsewhere.

You're allowed to make penalty-free withdrawals from traditional, spousal, and Roth IRAs for college costs or up to $10,000 for a down payment on your first home. But as I've stated before and will state again, it's usually unwise to raid your future reserves to pay for today's expenses. IRAs do not have a payback provision like 401(k)s, so withdrawals for even "good" purposes can set you back significantly.

Unless you have at least thirty years to aggressively rebuild your retirement savings, forgo all temptations to borrow or withdraw funds from 401(k)s and IRAs. Begin as early as you can and contribute as much as the law allows each year. Keep a good portion of your long-term savings in equity investments for growth, and watch the power of compounding work for you as you move closer to a financially independent retirement.

Now, Whatcha Gonna Do with All That Money?

Although this book has been about money and some of the Stupid Mistakes we make with it, I think it's important to wrap up our visit by emphasizing again that money is only a tool of life, not life itself. It's a means, not an end. But the truth is that when it comes time to shift gears from your full-time career to retirement, your financial condition is likely to be a key determining factor in the type of life you'll be able to enjoy. A healthy financial picture empowers you to keep your options open—free to travel, work part time, volunteer, go back to school, recreate, or pursue lifelong dreams.

It seems to me that the foundational question we're dealing with is not so much "How can I become financially independent for retirement?" as it is "How can I make the most of what I've got . . . to make the most of the rest of my life?" Retirement planning should not end with financial planning. Retirement planning also involves evaluating your attitudes, perhaps even rethinking your philosophy of retirement. After all, if you're going to spend up to one-third of your life there, why not plan on making those years some of the most productive, fulfilling times of your life?

It is for this reason that I've begun encouraging people to look upon their future retirement years as the New Retirement. Discard all the stereotypes of old age, Early Bird Specials, and frequent naps. Retirement is not the time to grow old, but to *grow*. Not the time to retreat, but to *rejuvenate*. Not the time to give up, but to *give back*. The New Retirement can be a take-charge time in which you proactively seek new challenges, learn new concepts, and delight in new discoveries. What a wonderful time in life to expand your computer skills, research and write your family history, design and tend a flower garden, learn a new language, read the classics, start a small business, explore and learn about nature, get another degree, improve a recreational skill, hike and camp and fish, read and study the Bible, start and maintain a journal of gratitude, learn photography or stained glass or floral design, attend seminars, and take educational tours. Retirement is not the time to grow old and retreat, but to grow and rejuvenate.

It's also a great time to reach out and give back. You can volunteer to help at your church or local outreaches; lead book-discussion clubs; teach a child a new skill; teach an adult to read; visit and encourage shut-ins and hospital patients; help at the local animal shelter; do housework or repairs for a disabled neighbor; volunteer at the local hospital or elder-care center; baby-sit, housesit, or pet-sit for friends who need to get away; deliver meals and cheer through Meals-On-Wheels; adopt a stretch of highway to keep tidy; life-coach a young adult; take your pet to hospitals, convalescent centers, or nursing homes to brighten patients' days; purchase and plant trees and flowers; write generous checks to worthy causes; make toys for ill children; write notes of encouragement; help rebuild a hiking trail; or take (and finance) a short-term mission. The possibilities are endless, and you can make a difference.

Financial independence is not the goal; it is simply a means to help free you from financial dependence on children, government, or charity. Free from worry, able to pay your own way and handle life's surprises. Free to give and share your time, talent, and treasure. Able to go where you want to go and do what you want to do. And, yes, free to take a nap.

Indeed, our retirement years can be the most fulfilling, productive time of our lives. Henry van Dyke's poem, "The Zest for Life," says it well:

> I shall grow old, but never lose life's zest,
> Because the road's last turn will be the best.

How To Secure Financial Freedom and Live Out Your Dreams.

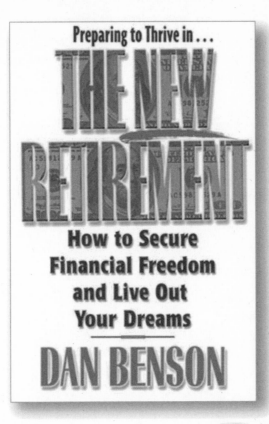

Preparing to Thrive in . . .

THE NEW RETIREMENT

How to Secure Financial Freedom and Live Out Your Dreams

DAN BENSON

In *The New Retirement*, Dan Benson helps you answer the question, "How do I make the money last while making the most of the rest of my life?" and puts you on the road to a financially free "New Retirement." Your future will seem brighter as you discover fresh, creative ways to become financially secure while staying young at heart, strong of body, and keen of mind.

W PUBLISHING GROUP™